MW01231654

Operation Iraqi Freedom

Operation Iraqi Freedom

A Strategic Assessment

Thomas Donnelly

The AEI Press

Publisher for the American Enterprise Institute

WASHINGTON, D.C.

Available in the United States from the AEI Press, c/o Client Distribution Services, 193 Edwards Drive, Jackson, TN 38301. To order, call toll free: 1-800-343-4499. Distributed outside the United States by arrangement with Eurospan, 3 Henrietta Street, London WC2E 8LU, England.

Library of Congress Cataloging-in-Publication Data

Donnelly, Thomas, 1953-
    Operation Iraqi Freedom: a strategic assessment / Thomas Donnelly.
       p. cm.
    Includes bibliographical references.
      ISBN 0-8447-4195-7 (pbk. : alk. paper)
      1. Iraq War, 2003. I. Title.

    DS79.76.D66 2004
    956.7044'3—dc22

                                       2004013262

10 09 08 07 06 05 04   1 2 3 4 5

Cover photograph caption: Two U.S. soldiers watch the area from the top of their headquarters in Falluja, November 2003.

© 2004 by the American Enterprise Institute for Public Policy Research, Washington, D.C. All rights reserved. No part of this publication may be used or reproduced in any manner whatsoever without permission in writing from the American Enterprise Institute except in the case of brief quotations embodied in news articles, critical articles, or reviews. The views expressed in the publications of the American Enterprise Institute are those of the authors and do not necessarily reflect the views of the staff, advisory panels, officers, or trustees of AEI.

Printed in the United States of America

Contents

Acknowledgments

This work, imperfect as it may be, would not have been possible but for the assistance and friendship of a great many people. I would particularly like to thank the members of the U.S. military who made my trip to Iraq in June and July 2003 so productive. My travel was purely unofficial, yet as always, soldiers, sailors, airmen, and marines went out of their way—without waiting for approval from Washington or Tampa—to get me where I wanted to go, give me a couch or a cot to sleep on and as many MREs as I could stand, and, most valuably, share their time and their stories. There are too many to thank individually, but I owe special debts to Lieutenant General David D. McKiernan and his staff, the staff of V Corps, and Lieutenant General David Petraeus and the troopers of the 101st Airborne Division. I also owe a debt of nearly two decades to retired General Carl Vuono, former chief of staff of the U.S. Army, and his personal staff, who gave me a truly superior military education.

A second group of friends and colleagues provided guidance and advice; some of them will be appalled at what I have made of their sage counsel, but they nonetheless deserve my gratitude. They include Andrew Bacevich of Boston University; Eliot Cohen of Johns Hopkins University School of Advanced International Studies; Peter Feaver of Duke University; military consultant Colonel Robert Killebrew, USA (Ret.); Thomas Keaney of Johns Hopkins University School of Advanced International Studies; Richard Kohn of the University of North Carolina; William Kristol of *The Weekly Standard*; my former colleague on the House Armed Services Committee staff, Jim Lariviere; my former colleague and coauthor at *Army Times*, Sean Naylor; Gary Schmitt at the Project for the New American Century; and Michael Vickers of the Center for Strategic and Budgetary Assessments. Further thanks are due to Steve

Metz of the U.S. Army War College and Andrew Krepinevich of the Center for Strategic and Budgetary Assessments, who provided valuable feedback on the draft of this report.

Finally, this report is not simply mine but a product of many people at the American Enterprise Institute. No scholar or writer works in a vacuum, and I am immensely grateful to AEI. Chris DeMuth and David Gerson perform a most mysterious magic—the care, feeding, and leading of an academic institution—with great aplomb. And last, but hardly least, something much more than thanks is due to my AEI colleagues who have worked with me on Iraq issues through the war: Danielle Pletka, Richard Perle, Reuel Marc Gerecht, Molly McKew, Katherine Smyth, Frances Tilney, and, in particular, Vance Serchuk.

THOMAS DONNELLY
American Enterprise Institute
June 2004

Executive Summary

More than a year after President Bush declared "mission accomplished" in the invasion of Iraq, a fuller victory in the war remains elusive. That is, in large part, because a fuller understanding of the war remains elusive. This report is an attempt to enlarge our understanding of Operation Iraqi Freedom, to point us in the right direction by analyzing where we have said we want to go and trying to find out where we are now. The report offers four key observations:

- The Iraq campaigns—both the conventional invasion to topple Saddam Hussein and the current counterinsurgency meant to provide security for the political reconstruction of Iraq—are just two parts of the so-called "war on terrorism." This war, properly understood, is a struggle to build a decent, more democratic and liberal, and less violent order throughout the "greater Middle East," that giant swath of the planet that extends from West Africa to Southeast Asia. The collapse of the traditional order, upon which past U.S. policies of containment and power-balancing rested, began twenty-five years ago, with the multiple crises of 1979. It required the attacks of September 11, 2001—and more importantly, the decisions made by President George W. Bush—to redirect American security and military strategy toward rebuilding the regional order to achieve a more durable peace.

- Military planning for the invasion did not fully reflect the administration's change of policy. In effect, President Bush asked for a campaign to achieve "regime change," but what he got was a campaign of "regime removal." This is not simply a scholastic distinction. Getting rid of Saddam and his henchmen was the easier part; replacing a well-entrenched dictatorship—in a region which knows little else—with a more representative form of government is proving to be, as Defense Secretary Donald Rumsfeld put it, a "long, hard slog." The Pentagon's desire to fight a rapid war undercut its ability to fight a decisive war.

- The conduct of the invasion shaped the difficulties of the counterinsurgency campaign. The "just-in-time" nature of the plan magnified the challenges of even relatively minor problems, such as the resistance of the Saddam fedayeen in the south of Iraq or the delays caused by an unexpectedly persistent sandstorm. And Turkey's failure to permit a northern invasion of Iraq contributed to the difficulties of projecting force beyond Baghdad, into the notorious "Sunni Triangle," the most significant area of resistance.

- The counterinsurgency, despite these troubles, has been remarkably successful. The two essential elements for completing the victory in Iraq, U.S. and Iraqi public opinion, have held firm despite the level of casualties and the missteps of the Bush administration. The insurgency has only succeeded in driving some lesser members of the international coalition out of the country; even the United Nations has returned to contribute to the reconstruction of Iraq.

Taken together, these four observations suggest that the Bush administration has charted the correct strategy in Iraq, but has failed to match its military means to its political ends. While the failure to provide adequate security has yet to prove fatal to the larger reconstruction mission in Iraq, the issue remains in doubt. It is uncertain whose side time is on, and the absence of a greater sense of urgency gives hope to the insurgents—whose first goal, after all, is simply to stave off defeat.

Most importantly, the administration seems not to appreciate President Bush's fundamental insight: In the effort to transform the greater Middle East, our security interests and our political principles are in alignment. As Andrew Krepinevich, executive director of the Center for Strategic and Budgetary Assessments, has observed, this struggle is a marathon, but we have a military—indeed, an entire national security bureaucracy—built for sprints. In Iraq and in the larger war, including in Afghanistan, the disparity between ends and means has begun to matter. We must either take the steps necessary to wage a long war or pursue a more limited victory. But that is simply a euphemism for defeat.

Prologue

The Road to Baghdad, 1991

On March 6, 1991, three days after signing a cease-fire ending Operation Desert Storm, General H. Norman Schwarzkopf awoke with the sinking feeling that he had been "suckered" by the Iraqi generals he had negotiated with at the border town of Safwan.

At the same time, President George H. W. Bush was basking in the glow of what seemed like a stunning victory. The one hundred–hour ground attack to evict the Iraqi army from Kuwait had been a smashing success; the number of U.S. casualties, amazingly low. Americans were jubilant and expectations were high that the troops, many of whom had been waiting in the Saudi desert for months, would soon be home. Yellow ribbons and plans for victory parades were in the air.

But Schwarzkopf's superiors in Washington were frustrated by Saddam Hussein's apparent recalcitrance in complying with the United Nations resolutions that governed the end of the campaign. Unsure of the situation, Schwarzkopf issued a demanding, almost contradictory set of orders to his principal subordinate, Lieutenant General John Yeosock. Yeosock's chief planner, Major General Steven Arnold, U.S. Central Command (CENTCOM), would continue to prepare for a rapid withdrawal from Iraq, the commander said, but in the meantime do not give up an inch of Iraqi territory. Leave the "minimum essential force" in place, he instructed.[1]

"Minimum essential force for what?" wondered Yeosock and Arnold. For the purpose, they inferred, of renewing an attack toward Baghdad, to remove Saddam Hussein and his regime from power.

"We had seen the reversal of [the directive] to get out of Iraq fast," recalled Arnold. By March 8, it seemed as though the cease-fire agreement was in deep trouble; the Iraqis were proving truculent on nearly every aspect of the deal, which in any event was a "cessation of hostilities," not a true peace or even a formal cease-fire. The next day, Arnold briefed Yeosock with what he called "a think piece," entitled "The Road to Baghdad." It was a plan to "speed up the peace process" by threatening Saddam and capturing—surrounding or "cordoning off," in more precise military terms—the Iraqi capital.

As the two generals and their immediate staff worked through the implications of the contingency plan, it became clearer that the distinction between "threatening" the regime and eliminating it was very slim, if not wholly illusory. With the armored forces of Saddam's Republican Guard badly damaged in Desert Storm, and with uprisings underway in northern and southern Iraq, the regime had moved its most loyal forces from their bases near Saddam's hometown of Tikrit down to Baghdad. The Iraqi dictator was scrambling to reorganize his scattered and battered army while suppressing the Kurds in the north and the Shi'a in the south. Saddam's grip on power was tenuous.

At the same time, the prospect of fighting in the streets of Baghdad was daunting. Yeosock had "liked the idea that we [had been] fighting in a big sandbox [during Desert Storm], clearly out of population centers. We had chosen to fight the war where there wasn't anybody but soldiers. That was no longer possible."

As the difference between threatening Saddam and overthrowing him collapsed, Arnold and Yeosock began to believe that a march on Baghdad would benefit from the Kurdish and Shi'a rebels. Arnold in particular felt that both groups would support any U.S. effort to topple Saddam. Yet both generals also remembered and accepted the Bush administration's policy of keeping Iraq intact and preserving it as a "counterweight" against a militantly revolutionary Iran. They assumed they would have to rebuild the Iraqi armed forces to provide both for internal stability and against external threats. It was clear to both that a move on Baghdad would require a long-term commitment of U.S. forces. And neither general wanted his troops to become an occupying army.

If the "Road to Baghdad" seemed sewn with political landmines, the military challenges seemed quite manageable. Arnold and his planning staff quickly came up with a variety of options involving a mixture of air power, airborne infantry, and armored punch. While a thrust toward Baghdad would cover hundreds of miles of tough terrain and require a significant force and long lines of communications, the task appeared to be well within the reach of the U.S. force still in Iraq. While Arnold was reluctant to commit conventional forces into potentially dangerous urban combat, it was more than possible to destroy or outmaneuver the remnants of the Iraqi army—especially in the midst of the ongoing rebellion. While no cakewalk, the road to Baghdad was clear. As Arnold put it,

> We could certainly get to Baghdad and there were several options to get there. But we certainly wouldn't expect to do that without wholehearted Arab support and approval. Once there, we recommended that we not be the ones to do the house-to-house search for Saddam. . . . It was clearly in my mind that the best possible outcome was [that] we would go up to Baghdad and the government would fall and we would let some element unknown to me become the new government and we would quickly withdraw and everybody would be happy. That was the rosiest scenario.

> The other extreme would be [that] we would go to Baghdad and take it, the government would withdraw into northern Iraq, hide, and a never-ending guerrilla war would result. We felt the most probable [outcome] was somewhere in between. We would be able to set up a new government, but we probably wouldn't be able to withdraw for some time. My guess is that [Saddam] would run and hide and we probably had a 50-50 chance of getting him. It would be like [trying to find Panamanian leader Manuel] Noriega, tenfold. It would be a hard mission and you would need some contact inside the Iraqi structure to help you. . . . You're talking about a pretty long-term commitment.[2]

But the prospect of a march on Baghdad faded as quickly as it appeared. The Bush administration hoped that the Kurdish and Shi'a uprisings would topple Saddam, but was reluctant to intervene. "The impetus [again] became, how fast can you get [American troops] out of there and are we going to get them all back for the Washington parade or the New York parade, [the] Fourth of July," remembered Yeosock. "How fast can you get out of Iraq so that we can get the United Nations to help?" After a formal review of Arnold's contingency plan on March 19, Yeosock concluded: "Put it on ice."

Months later, Yeosock recalled the moment: "See, everybody is happy. Yellow ribbons are out, flags are flying. CENTCOM went home. Now it's the end of this thing. A lot of people don't understand that sometimes the hardest part is the beginning and the end."

PART I

The Political and Strategic Setting

It is impossible to understand American decisions about Saddam Hussein—to support him in power after the Islamist revolution in Iran, to leave him in power after the Gulf War, to remove him from power after the September 11 attacks, and, most crucially, to supplant him in power with an experiment in Arab democracy—without understanding American policy toward the Middle East. Iraq, in short, has always been a piece of a larger puzzle. This report will attempt not only to clarify what happened on the battlefield during Operation Iraqi Freedom, but also to place the tactical and operational aspects of that conflict into the broader context of American grand strategy in the Middle East.

The report begins with a review of past U.S. policies in the Middle East and notes the deepening engagement of U.S. military forces in the region over the past twenty-five years. This is the context for a close examination of the planning for the Iraq war—both the invasion and toppling of the government of Saddam Hussein, and the extended counterinsurgency campaign that has marked the initial effort to secure the conditions for the political and economic reconstruction of Iraq. The report continues with an analysis of the strategic and military implications of the war. The report is thus part narrative—an attempt to come to a coherent understanding of what happened—and part assessment—an attempt to explain why things happened as they did, and what their larger meaning might be.

For much of its history as a world power, and especially during the decades of the Cold War, the United States sought to preserve the political order of the greater Middle East, as roughly established in the aftermath of World War I. Like Britain a hundred years before, twentieth-century America used its political, economic, and military might to prop up an array of native regimes, usually of questionable political and moral legitimacy. This strategy, known as "offshore balancing," kept the United States engaged, but at a distance, juggling proxies to ensure that oil kept flowing out and to prevent the Soviets from pushing in.

This balancing act was an inherently delicate one, as various local powers plied both sides of the Cold War contest for favors. And when the system finally began to unravel, for reasons both internal and external to the Middle East, American power was dragged into the region as never before.

The process by which the United States moved from a strategy of offshore balancing to direct intervention, from seeking to preserve the status quo in the Middle East to radically remaking it, is intrinsically tied to Saddam Hussein and, more broadly, the events of 1979. It was during this tumultuous year that the disintegration of the old political order in the Middle East began to accelerate, with Saddam openly coming to power in Baghdad, the Islamist revolution toppling the shah in Iran, and the Soviet Union invading Afghanistan. In addition, in late November, a cell of Saudi Arabian dissidents seized control of the Grand Mosque in Mecca, killing dozens of pilgrims while denouncing the Saudi royal family for its dissolute and Westernized ways. The group's leader, Juhayman al-Utaybi, called for the "purification of Islam" and the overthrow of the House of Saud.[1] Once the immediate crisis passed, Saudi leaders worked furiously to tighten their links to the extreme Wahhabi clerics that had long been key to the regime's power. In many ways, what 1914 was to the old order in Europe, 1979 would be to the old order in the Middle East.

At the time, of course, the overthrow of the shah and the invasion of Afghanistan appeared to be of vastly greater urgency than events in Iraq or Saudi Arabia. In hindsight, the former crises are notable foremost for pushing the White House and the Pentagon toward establishing significant, conventional military capabilities in the Persian Gulf—a strategic development that would prove to be of far more lasting importance than either the funding of the *mujahideen* or the failed "Desert One" raid. In January 1980, a month after the Soviet invasion of Afghanistan, President Carter bluntly articulated America's willingness to intervene militarily in the Middle East in his State of the Union address:

> Let our position be absolutely clear: An attempt by any outside force to gain control of the Persian Gulf region will be regarded

as an assault on the vital interests of the United States of America, and such an assault will be repelled by any means necessary, including military force.[2]

To give substance to this declaration, the president authorized the creation of a Rapid Deployment Joint Task Force, an ad hoc military organization that would later be formalized by President Ronald Reagan in 1983 as U.S. Central Command. As Carter speechwriter Hendrik Hertzberg recalled: "We knew that we didn't really have the teeth to back up the [threat of force in the Middle East]. We had nuclear weapons, but not the conventional forces to make it stick if the Soviets chose to challenge it."[3]

U.S. Central Command did not play a significant interventionist role in the Middle East during the 1980s, directing its attention more toward Libyan-led insurrections in Africa. While fully committed to "rolling back" the Soviet empire on its vulnerable frontiers in Eastern Europe, the Reagan administration more or less maintained the strategy of offshore balancing it had inherited in the Middle East, fighting the Iranians and the Soviets through intermediaries. Ironically, when the Pentagon would finally be called upon to fight a conventional war in the Persian Gulf, it would not be against America's traditional foes in the region, but Iraq.

In this regard, it was the rise of Saddam more than anything else that would bring a formal end to offshore balancing. Saddam's rise was predicated and sustained by violence—violence against his neighbors and violence against fellow Iraqis—on a scale that was striking even by the sanguinary standards of the modern Middle East. Specifically, it was through the bloody upheaval of the Iran-Iraq war that the traditional balance of military power in the Middle East collapsed.

None of this, of course, was readily apparent to American policymakers on September 22, 1980, when Iraq launched a small-scale offensive against the Iranian city of Khoramshahr. Saddam evidently expected a "splendid little war," in which his swift capture of Iranian territory would lead to negotiations with Ayatollah Khomeini or to the collapse of the Islamist regime. Neither happened. Instead, Saddam inadvertently set into motion a series of events that would destroy the balance-of-power basis for a half century of American policy in the region.

Initially, the U.S. foreign policy establishment seemed to care little about what promised to be a limited struggle between a radical Islamic theocracy and a Soviet client state. "It is too bad they both can't lose," quipped former secretary of state Henry Kissinger.[4] But Iran's series of battlefield victories and Khomeini's expanded war aims soon startled the United States. In keeping with the long-standing strategy of offshore balancing, the Reagan administration began to view Iraq—noxious though Saddam was—as a *de facto* buffer against the spread of Islamic fundamentalism in the Persian Gulf.

By March 1982, fear of revolutionary Iran had sufficiently outstripped fear of Saddam's Iraq that the Reagan administration removed Iraq from the official State Department list of state sponsors of terrorism. But, as a Defense Department official explained, "No one had any doubts about [the Iraqis'] continued involvement in terrorism. . . . The real reason was to help them succeed in the war against Iran."[5]

Iraq's defenses were stiffened by help from the United States, notably an intelligence-sharing agreement in 1984. It was a move that "analysts would later describe as having saved the Iraqis from being overrun in several key battles."[6] After the 1984 election, the Reagan administration pursued even closer ties with Saddam, in particular by subsidizing purchases of American agricultural products, since Iraq could no longer feed itself or its growing army. And over the strenuous objections of then assistant secretary of defense Richard Perle,

> [T]he United States sold to Iraq a wide variety of "dual-use" items. For instance, Iraq purchased more than 100 helicopters from manufacturers in the United States, which in export documents were designated for civilian and recreational purposes. Upon arrival in Iraq they immediately were diverted to the front with Iran, with no protest from Washington.[7]

In part because of U.S. assistance, Saddam's regime weathered the Iranian onslaught, but it took until the summer of 1988 before the conditions were ripe for a negotiated settlement. Ultimately, the eight-year war—at a cost of over one million lives—had almost no direct territorial consequence. It ended with a return to the previous international border, and both the Iranian Islamic regime and the Ba'ath Party remained in power.

Yet the strategic balance in the region was forever altered. Iran had been broken as a conventional military power, while Iraq had been transformed from a police state into a military state; its army had gone from 180,000 men—1 percent of the population—to roughly one million men—about 6 percent of the population, a level of mobilization that surpassed that of the Union during the American Civil War. The previous "natural balance" between Iraq and Iran had also been undermined by Saudi Arabia, a huge source of funding for Iraq as well as the anti-Soviet forces in Afghanistan. Leveraging the influence that flowed from its incredible oil wealth, the Saudis were coming to play a strategic role its small population and traditional society could otherwise not sustain.

American policy, nonetheless, remained focused on the threat of revolutionary Iran, with the Bush administration determined to make Baghdad its partner in Gulf security. Even as it acknowledged the mismatch between the broken Iraqi economy and the huge military machine Saddam had built, the U.S. foreign policy establishment imagined that Iraq was exhausted after the long struggle with Iran. A 1989 Pentagon paper acknowledged Iraq's use of chemical weapons as well as its nuclear ambitions, and noted that it "had emerged from the Iran-Iraq war with the largest, most-experienced and best-equipped standing armed forces in the Arab world." But the paper concluded optimistically that "warweary" Iraq would "be reluctant to engage in foreign military adventures. It is more likely to resort to diplomacy and subversion to achieve its goals. Attacks against U.S. forces coming to the aid of U.S. allies in the region are unlikely."[8]

In October 1989, President George H. W. Bush took another step toward a closer relationship with Saddam Hussein, in a new national security directive. "NSD-26" concluded that the United States "should propose economic and political incentives for Iraq to moderate its behavior." In addition to close economic ties, the first Bush administration was ready for open military-to-military exchanges, "as a means of developing access to an influence with the Iraqi defense establishment." All of this was, of course, justified by the realist, balance-of-power mindset that governed U.S. policy in the region: "Normal relations between the United

States and Iraq would serve our longer-term interests and promote stability both in the Gulf and the Middle East."9

Indeed, this continued to be the directive and theory for the Bush administration's Iraq policy up until the 1990 invasion of Kuwait. To be sure, U.S. intelligence agencies chronicled the Iraqi military's deployment of Scud ballistic missiles, the genocidal campaign against the Iraqi Kurds, and the collapse of the Iraqi economy; and the Pentagon, particularly U.S. Central Command, began to shift the focus of its war-planning from Iran to Iraq, especially as the rhetoric of the Iraqi regime grew bellicose. When the Scuds were redeployed to western Iraq, for instance, Saddam delivered a speech promising to "make fire eat up half of Israel."10 But not even the gathering threat to Kuwait could convince the Bush administration that Saddam was a dangerous bedfellow.

As Republican Guard tanks amassed along the Kuwaiti border in late July 1990, Saddam told U.S. ambassador April Glaspie, "Yours is a society that cannot accept 10,000 dead in one battle." Glaspie's infamous response: "We have no opinion on the Arab-Arab conflicts like your border disagreement with Kuwait. . . . [Secretary of State] James Baker has directed our official spokesman to emphasize this instruction."11

The 1991 Gulf War

Indeed, the invasion of Kuwait did not force a fundamental reevaluation of U.S. security strategy in the Persian Gulf or the Islamic world more broadly; operations Desert Shield and Desert Storm were, ultimately, an attempt to reestablish a balance of power in the region. In convincing the Saudi royal family that it should agree to the deployment of American soldiers to defend its country, then secretary of defense Richard Cheney reported to King Fahd, "The president asked me to assure you that we will stay as long as you want us. We will stay until justice is done but not stay a minute longer."12 As the defense of Saudi Arabia was ensured and the administration began to consider offensive operations, the questions were more about exit strategies, casualties, and other factors that would limit the risks of a war. Colin Powell, then chairman of the Joint Chiefs of Staff, captured the mood well in his subsequent autobiography: "Do we want to go beyond Kuwait to Baghdad? Do we try to force Saddam out of power? How weakened do we want to leave Iraq? Do we necessarily benefit from a Gulf oil region dominated by an unfriendly Syria and a hostile Iran?"[13] In the minds of the senior leaders of the first Bush administration, the answer to each of these questions was clearly, "*No.*"

Thus, President Bush put forward a limited set of objectives: "The immediate, complete and unconditional withdrawal of all Iraqi forces from Kuwait; the restoration of Kuwait's legitimate government."[14] This was a definition of the war the rest of the world (including the failing regime of Mikhail Gorbachev and eventually even Hafez al-Assad's Syria) could live with. Beating Saddam's legions back across the border would reestablish the old order, not create a new one.

But these limited aims could not answer many of the questions that arose from the triumph of Operation Desert Storm. Without doubt, the president's narrow definition of victory had been achieved in remarkable style, with very few U.S. casualties. Yet the restoration of the Kuwaiti government and the damage inflicted upon the Iraqi army neither resulted in the fall of Saddam Hussein nor restored the basis for a balance-of-power security policy in the Middle East. The key decision makers in the first Bush administration were adamant about their decision to avoid a deeper American involvement in the region, as their collective memoirs reveal. Wrote General Norman Schwarzkopf, head of U.S. Central Command during the war:

> Despite all of the so-called "experts" who, with twenty-twenty hindsight, are now criticizing that "decision," at the time the war ended there was not a single head of state, diplomat, Middle East expert, or military leader who, as far as I am aware, advocated continuing the war and seizing Baghdad. The United Nations resolutions that provided the legal basis for our military operations in the gulf were clear in their intent: kick the Iraqi military force out of Kuwait. We had authority to take whatever actions were necessary to accomplish that mission, including attacks into Iraq, but we had no authority to invade Iraq for the purpose of capturing the entire country or its capital. . . .

Had the United States and the United Kingdom gone on alone to capture Baghdad, under the provisions of the Geneva and Hague conventions we would have been considered occupying powers and therefore would have been responsible for *all* the costs of maintaining or restoring government, education, and other services for the people of Iraq. From the brief time we did spend occupying Iraqi territory after the war, I am certain that had we taken all of Iraq, we would have been like the dinosaur in the tar pit—we would still be there, and we, not the United Nations, would be bearing the costs of that occupation.[15]

Schwarzkopf's superiors agreed. In his autobiography, Powell outlined the nature of U.S. strategy: "Our practical intention was to leave Baghdad enough power to survive as a threat to an Iran that remained bitterly hostile to the United States."[16] Quoting historian John Keegan, Powell insisted that Desert Storm fulfilled "the highest purpose of military action: the use of force in the cause of order."[17] In their memoir, *A World Transformed*, President Bush and his national security advisor, Brent Scowcroft, made clear that regional stability in the Persian Gulf and the Middle East was the primary goal. Otherwise, wrote Bush and Scowcroft, "We would be committing ourselves—alone—to removing one regime and installing another. . . . We would be facing some dubious 'nation-building.'"[18] The notion of a "desert democracy," as Powell put it, was "naïve."[19]

The first Bush administration's approach to Iraq was consistent with its overall security policy and its approach to managing the disintegration of the Soviet Union; it tended to fret about the collapse of old power balances rather than to celebrate the liberty of formerly captive nations. Additionally, the Middle East was still a strategic battlefield secondary to Europe (as was East Asia, as indicated by the administration's response to the 1989 Tiananmen Square massacre). And with Saddam Hussein so weakened, containment scored some initial successes. In particular, United Nations (UN) weapons inspectors made significant inroads exposing Iraq's weapons of mass destruction (WMD) programs, which proved to be far more advanced than thought before the war, while the sanctions imposed by UN Resolution 687 frustrated Saddam's efforts to reconstitute his conventional force. To protect the Kurds and Shi'a from further large-scale attacks and the strafing of helicopter gunships (a measure unwittingly agreed to by Schwarzkopf at the Desert Storm cease-fire meeting), so-called "no-fly" zones were belatedly established over northern and southern Iraq and patrolled by U.S., British, and French aircraft.

Yet Saddam soon began to push back. In late 1992, provocations in the southern no-fly zone provoked harsh and unanimous rebukes from the United States, Britain, France, and Russia. When Saddam shifted tactics in January 1993, attempting to impede weapons inspections and illegally repossess equipment abandoned in Kuwait, the UN declared Iraq in material breach of the cease-fire resolution. On January 13, over one hundred American, French, and British aircraft hit targets across southern Iraq, and four days after that, the United States fired forty-five Tomahawk missiles against the Zafaraniyah nuclear weapons complex outside Baghdad. Baghdad subsequently announced a "cease-fire."

Still, these attacks—President Bush's parting gift to Saddam Hussein—set an unfortunate precedent for the next administration's Iraq policy. As Michael Gordon of the *New York Times* reported at the time, "The style of the allied military attacks communicated caution as much as strength. The first attack . . . was compressed into 15 minutes. By limiting that attack to a single, brief raid, the allies missed three of the four surface-to-air-missile batteries they tried to destroy, forcing them to go back almost a week later to hit the targets again."[20]

Containment under Clinton

In the 1992 presidential campaign, candidate Bill Clinton attacked the Bush administration for having failed to learn from its appeasement of Saddam Hussein and for having "left the Kurds and the Shi'ites twisting."[21] A Clinton administration, by contrast, would not "forge strategic relationships with dangerous, despotic regimes." Instead, the Arkansas governor pledged that his administration would "contain" Saddam while supporting the Iraqi opposition forces that the Bush administration had pointedly ignored:

In August 1993, Vice President Gore wrote to the Iraqi National Congress affirming America's "solid commitment" to "your struggle" and pledging that the Clinton team "will not turn our backs" because "our purpose . . . is to establish clearly and unequivocally that the current regime in Iraq is a criminal regime, beyond the pale of international society and, in our judgment, irredeemable."[22]

William Jefferson Clinton was inaugurated as the forty-second president of the United States with a plan "to focus like a laser beam on the economy." In sharp contrast to his predecessor, America's new commander-in-chief professed disinterest in international relations. "I might have to spend all of my time on foreign policy, and I don't want that to happen," he worried.[23] To the extent that it paid attention to the subject, the Clinton administration was animated by the lofty ideals of international cooperation, sustainable development, and collective security. "We have learned that the world works better when differences are resolved by force of argument rather than force of arms," Clinton explained.[24]

In keeping with this view, the United States would direct its energies in the Middle East toward peacemaking rather than power politics. In particular, Clinton believed that the collapse of the Soviet Union had created a "window of opportunity" to negotiate a lasting peace in the Israeli-Palestinian conflict.[25] As for Iraq, a showdown with Saddam was not in the cards.

Yet Saddam Hussein was not content to let the Clinton administration push him to the sidelines of history. In April 1993, just days before George H. W. Bush's visit to Kuwait to commemorate the end of the first Gulf War, the Kuwaiti government uncovered an Iraqi plot to assassinate the former American president and the emir of Kuwait. A group of Iraqi and Kuwait nationals was arrested—one of whom confessed that he had been dispatched by Iraqi intelligence—and a 200-pound bomb was discovered in a car that had been driven across the border from Iraq into Kuwait.

In the face of this narrowly thwarted act of terrorism, the Clinton administration fired twenty-three Tomahawk cruise missiles at Iraqi intelligence headquarters. The bombing was conducted in the dead of the night against an essentially deserted target. Although only modestly damaging to Iraqi intelligence-gathering capabilities, this pinprick strike was trumpeted by the administration as an important blow against Saddam Hussein. Two days later, Clinton announced to his Cabinet that they had "cripple[d] the Iraqi intelligence capacity." He then added, "I think it's very important today at this Cabinet meeting that we . . . get back to the domestic agenda."[26]

President Clinton hoped that the attack against Iraqi intelligence headquarters would demonstrate to Baghdad the futility of pursuing hegemonic ambitions, whether through conventional military means or acts of terrorism. And indeed, the Tomahawk raids did push Saddam away from active confrontation with the United States—albeit with the perverse consequence that his efforts focused instead on misleading UN weapons inspectors and wooing America's erstwhile allies. Soon, the United Nations Special Commission (UNSCOM) and the International Atomic Energy Agency (IAEA) began to hint that active inspections might no longer be necessary, while the Russian government floated a proposal before the Security Council to set a date for the lifting of sanctions.

When the United States fended off these attempts to rehabilitate Saddam Hussein, the dictator returned to more aggressive forms of resistance. By 1994, the worsening economic situation in Iraq translated into widespread unrest, including two assassination attempts against Saddam in as many months. Faced with bleak prospects, Baghdad upped the ante in early October by deploying troops to the Kuwaiti border and demanding that the United Nations lift sanctions at the next periodic review session, scheduled for October 10.

The Clinton administration's response to this provocation was purely defensive. Operation Vigilant Warrior was a massive reinforcement of the U.S. military presence in the region, raising American troop strength in the Gulf from 13,000 to approximately 60,000, including an 18,000-strong Marine Expeditionary Force, a carrier group, and 350 additional aircraft. Britain also dispatched its own vessels and aircraft, while France sent a frigate as a sign of solidarity. The UN Security Council subsequently passed Resolution 949, requiring Baghdad to remove its forces from southern Iraq and refrain from any future deployments south of the 32nd Parallel.

Although Operation Vigilant Warrior effectively deterred Saddam Hussein from an act of international aggression, it also demonstrated

America's reluctance to move directly against the despot on his own turf—a tendency that was only strengthened in the aftermath of the CIA's disastrously mismanaged covert operation against Saddam in March 1995. As President Clinton later explained, "Our ability to control internal events in Iraq is limited."[27]

The full extent of these limitations was revealed in December 1994, after the chief of the Iraqi intelligence services, Wafiq al-Samarra'i, defected. In his debriefing, he claimed that UNSCOM had been wildly misled by the regime; that Iraq had manufactured and loaded VX nerve agent onto missiles during the Gulf War; that it had a far more comprehensive and intact biological warfare program than the inspectors realized; and that it had secreted biological and chemical munitions, along with over forty modified Scud ballistic missiles, since then. These accusations about Iraq's WMD programs were later reiterated by Saddam Hussein's son-in-law, Hussein Kamel, after he defected to Jordan the next year.

It was also in 1995 that the UN Security Council unanimously adopted Resolution 986, providing for a system whereby Iraq could sell $2 billion worth of oil every six months to pay for food and other humanitarian supplies. The proposal effectively undermined Saddam Hussein's demand that sanctions be lifted for reasons of "humanitarianism," especially after Iraq rejected the resolution.

Thus, by the second half of President Clinton's first term, certain facts were clear: Iraq continued to flaunt the will of the international community, ignoring the resolutions of the UN Security Council and repeatedly moving to the brink of war; high-level defectors indicated that Saddam Hussein's regime was continuing to pursue weapons of mass destruction under the noses of UN inspectors; the Iraqi people were suffering from a humanitarian catastrophe that Saddam Hussein was manipulating and perpetuating in a brutal bid to maintain his grip on power; and certain Arab allies, such as the king of Jordan, had indicated support for regime change in Baghdad.

Although some in the Clinton administration argued that the United States should take advantage of Saddam's moment of weakness and act against him, Secretary of State Warren Christopher argued that the current state of affairs, by virtue of keeping Saddam from threatening the stability of the region at minimal cost, was more than sufficient. In light of the administration's commitments to the Israeli-Palestinian peace process and the violence in the former Yugoslavia, Iraq was a relatively low priority.

And so it went. In what was by now a predictable pattern, Iraq again blocked UN weapons inspectors from entering a number of suspicious sites in June 1996. Although a minority in the administration considered this obstructionism to be grounds for the use of military force, they were undercut by UNSCOM Chairman Rolf Ekeus, who flew to Baghdad and negotiated a new agreement on inspections. The terms listed sixty "sensitive sites" to which UNSCOM could bring a team of four people, who would be escorted by an Iraqi "senior official." The Clinton administration acknowledged that Ekeus's concessions compromised the inspections process to the point of irrelevance. The pretense of regional unity against Saddam would be next to collapse.

In the summer of 1996, Saddam took advantage of the Kurdish civil war to redeploy Iraqi troops northward. Faced with a clear violation of the 1991 cease-fire agreement, Secretary of Defense William Perry flew to the Middle East to build consensus for air strikes, but encountered stiff resistance from Saudi Arabia and Turkey. As a result, the United States and Britain were forced to redraw the boundaries of the southern no-fly zone and to launch strikes out of that compromise on September 3–4, 1996.

While the strikes had the desired effect of halting Iraqi operations in Kurdistan, the episode highlighted the Clinton administration's inability to sustain the regional security framework against Saddam. In addition, initial Iraqi victories against the Kurds fortified Saddam's dominant position in the morass of Iraqi domestic politics. As a result, he accepted Resolution 986's "oil-for-food" program, prompting King Hussein of Jordan to withdraw his support for regime change. The window of opportunity had closed.

Over the next two years, Saddam's strength only grew. He learned to play the oil-for-food program for political advantage—as he had the humanitarian crisis before it—while sapping international resolve with the promise of lucrative contracts with a resource-rich and weapons-hungry state. When Rolf Ekeus was replaced by Richard Butler at UNSCOM, the Iraqis stepped up their harassment of inspectors, repeatedly tampering with transport arrangements, firing a rocket-propelled grenade into UN-SCOM headquarters in Baghdad in January 1998, and blocking a surprise inspection that fall.

In the midst of this heightened intransigence, the UN Security Council passed Resolution 1134 on October 23, 1997, threatening to restrict travel freedoms for Iraqi officials. The measure amounted to nothing more than a slap on the wrist—yet five members of the Security Council nonetheless abstained from the vote, including France, Russia, and China. This, predictably, roused Saddam to further obstructions, such as declaring that Iraq would withdraw from the oil-for-food program if negotiations on the removal of sanctions did not take place. The United States and Britain, after beginning to mass their forces in the region, then submitted to a Russian-brokered compromise. In January 1998, the sanctions deadlock was again replayed, only to be resolved this time by UN Secretary-General Kofi Annan, who traveled to Baghdad to broker yet another compromise with Iraq.

With the Clinton administration distracted by the Monica Lewinsky scandal and the al Qaeda bombings in Africa in 1998, Saddam mounted a new campaign against the UN inspectors, successfully driving them from the country. When the United States and Britain retaliated—Operation Desert Fox in December 1998—it was a four-day campaign that bolstered the coalition force posture in the region but did little else besides. The Omani newspaper *Al-Watan* correctly summarized the immediate impact of the air strikes as having "failed to weaken Saddam Hussein internally and increased his popularity among the Arabs."[28] Even more ominously, Desert Fox revealed that the Western and Arab "allies" of the United States and Britain had now become dead set against *any* military action against Iraq. Italy, France, and the Netherlands denounced the attacks and harbored protests, demonstrating the complete lack of cohesion of an international or UN-sanctioned strategy.[29]

Although the tortuous series of events that culminated in Desert Fox had convinced the administration that the only practical solution to the Iraq issue was a full change in the regime—President Clinton acknowledged as much during a radio address on the final day of the Desert Fox strikes—it was unwilling to act. There were, of course, countless excuses: The American public would not support a full-scale invasion; the CIA, burned by its previous stab at regime change in the mid-1990s, was adamantly opposed to the use of any proxy forces; and besides, the Iraqi opposition was as fragmented as ever. Another distraction came in the form of the war in Kosovo, and by the end of the NATO campaign there, the administration was assessing its exit strategy from the stage of history, hoping to peg its Middle Eastern legacy on the high note of Arab-Israeli peace rather than a messy invasion of Iraq.

Smart Sanctions and Containment, "W" Style

As a candidate for president in 2000, George W. Bush was, if anything, less interested in national security issues than Bill Clinton had been in 1992. As the governor of Texas, he could claim some knowledge of Latin American affairs, but his most memorable "gaffe" during the campaign was his failure to remember the name of General Pervez Musharraf, the president of Pakistan, when quizzed by a newspaper reporter. What emerged in two carefully scripted speeches given early in the race, one on defense policy at the Citadel in September 1999 and a second, more over-arching speech at the Reagan Library in November, was a mix of neocon-servative Reaganism and Kissingerian realism.[30]

This made for a certain Polonius-like quality that begged more ques-tions than it answered. "Let us reject the blinders of isolationism, just as we refuse the crown of empire," Bush said at the Reagan Library. "Let us not dominate others with our power, or betray them with our indiffer-ence. And let us have an American foreign policy that reflects American character. The modesty of true strength. The humility of real greatness. This is the strong heart of America," he concluded.[31]

As the campaign developed, candidate Bush and his foreign-policy "Vulcans"—a core of analysts with ties to the first Bush administration—tended to veer toward the realist pole, sharply criticizing the Clinton administration for its mushy multilateralism, military weakness, and predilection for "nation-building." Condoleezza Rice, now national secu-rity adviser and a protégé of Brent Scowcroft, proposed a "division of labor" among NATO members in the Balkans. "When it comes to nation-building or civilian administration or indefinite peacekeeping, we do need for the Europeans to step up to their responsibilities," she told the *New York Times*. "We don't need to have the 82nd Airborne escorting kids to kindergarten."[32]

The general view of the Bush campaign was that the United States should confine itself to managing the global balance of power and maintain the geopolitical status quo. As Rice explained on the eve of the 2000 election, "The United States is the only power that can handle a showdown in the [Persian] Gulf, mount the kind of force that is needed to protect Saudi Arabia and deter a crisis in the Taiwan Straits. Extended peacekeeping detracts from our readiness for these kinds of global missions."[33]

The note of humility in Bush's Reagan Library speech was more often sounded than the call to greatness. "If we're an arrogant nation, [the international community will] resent us," Bush said. "If we're a humble nation but strong, they'll welcome us. We've got to be humble yet project strength in a way that promotes freedom."[34] During the October 10, 2000, debate with Vice President Al Gore, Bush emphasized the need for strategic "humility" five times, and derided the idea of nation-building eight times.[35] Zalmay Khalizad, later President Bush's special envoy to Afghanistan and the Iraqi opposition, described a strategy of "selective global leadership"—implying that the sole superpower could choose to exercise its primacy where and when it wished, avoiding the kinds of constabulary missions that had marked the Clinton years. Human conflict might be inevitable, but the United States would pick its fights sparingly, choosing the ground and circumstances under which it would become involved.

During its early months in office, the Bush administration continued to emphasize the need to husband American strength, although the president himself, especially in unscripted moments, occasionally displayed an assertive streak, such as when he promised to defend Taiwan "whatever it takes" or threatened to reverse Clinton-era policy toward North Korea.[36] Just after assuming the presidency, Bush authorized a punitive cruise missile strike against Iraq very similar to the periodic "pinprick" attacks of the Clinton administration. The administration's main Iraq initiative was to revise the UN sanctions regime; Secretary of State Colin Powell called for "smart sanctions" that would better target Iraq's efforts to rebuild its military and weapons of mass destruction programs while finding ways to ease the suffering of the Iraqi people. Yet in practice, it was immediately clear that this was a doomed effort to maintain a coalition that already had collapsed; France, Russia, and China—all permanent members of the UN Security Council—wanted no part of the plan.

The Bush team also resisted any impulse to formulate a comprehensive national-security strategy or doctrine. The Pentagon's 2001 Quadrennial Defense Review (QDR), mandated by law, served as a substitute. Although the QDR, like many of its predecessors, resulted in a compromise solution dictated in part by internal Defense Department bureaucratic politics, it also marked a significant shift in military planning in discarding the post–Cold War benchmark for sizing U.S. forces: the ability to fight and win two large "theater wars" at the same time. Those who shaped the report generally agreed that the absence of great-power rivalry would create a period of "strategic pause" lasting several decades, or however long it might take the Chinese to become a "global peer competitor." This in turn would allow the United States to "transform" its military to exploit a "revolution in military affairs" brought on by the widespread application of information and other emerging technologies to weapons systems and a corresponding shift in tactics and organization. Despite the review's assertion that the administration intended to preserve U.S. military supremacy over the long term, the Pentagon leadership hoped, as President Bush had said, to "skip a generation" of procurement. It also seemed to want to skip a generation's worth of unappealing constabulary missions.

The Making of the Bush Doctrine

September 11, 2001, changed all that. Most importantly, it changed the mind of President Bush, who seems to have intuited from the first that the attacks were an act of war, not a crime, and that the "war" would be a struggle, primarily, to confront the myriad political problems of the Islamic world—the "greater Middle East" centered in the Arab heartland but stretching west into Africa and east through Central Asia to the Pacific.

There was no elaborate policy review. Instead, there was a presidential moment of clarity. Aboard Air Force One, watching the second of the twin towers collapse on television, President Bush thought "about the consequences of what had taken place. . . . I didn't need any legal briefs, I didn't need any consultations. I knew we were at war."[37]

What followed, for the next year and a half, through the prosecution of Operation Enduring Freedom in Afghanistan and in the run-up to Operation Iraqi Freedom, was the translation of the president's initial reaction into a fragmentary strategy largely through the vehicle of speechmaking. What emerged, known commonly as the "Bush Doctrine," has challenged many decades of American strategy and policy toward Iraq and the Middle East.

It has been a piecemeal process. By September 20, 2001, when he addressed a joint session of Congress, President Bush began the process of taking the nation to war as he saw it, a large and long war, not simply with a particular group of terrorists directly responsible for the attacks, but with "every terrorist group of global reach" and with the "nations that provide safe haven to terrorism."[38]

Over the subsequent months, the president's views of what he called "our mission and our moment" progressed. On November 6, 2001, he assured the Warsaw Conference on Combating Terrorism that the United States would wage war on terror "until we're rid of it." He also saw the potential threat of terrorists armed with chemical, biological, radiological, or nuclear weapons: "We will not wait for the authors of mass murder to gain weapons of mass destruction."[39] And shortly afterward, the president expanded his emphasis from terrorist groups to terror-loving states: "If you develop weapons of mass destruction [with which] you want to terrorize the world, you'll be held accountable."[40]

The January 29, 2002, State of the Union address marked the maturation of the Bush Doctrine. This war, according to the president, has "two great objectives." The first is defeating terrorism *per se*. The second objective marked an unequivocal rejection of the international status quo. "The United States of America," said President Bush, "will not permit the world's most dangerous regimes to threaten us with the world's most destructive weapons." He singled out three regimes—North Korea, Iran, and Iraq—as enemies; they constituted an "axis of evil" that posed "a grave and growing danger." Nor would his administration "stand by, as peril draws closer and closer." Time, he said, "is not on our side." The president foresaw the need to act preemptively and unilaterally under certain circumstances.[41]

Bush rooted his objection to the status quo in America's founding political principles. He would be leading a war for a democratic revolution, to remove tyrannical regimes. In this war on terrorism, "no nation is exempt," the president said, from the universal, "true and unchanging" American principles of liberty and justice. He saw these as "non-negotiable demands" that form the "greater objective" of the war.[42]

Through the spring of 2002, this resulted in new directions for American strategy, particularly in the Middle East. After the success in Afghanistan, Iraq became the primary object of attention; the administration talked openly of regime change in Baghdad and reversed a decade of policy in the Middle East centered on the Israeli-Palestinian "peace process." Hereafter, U.S. policy would insist upon democratization as a prerequisite for Palestinian statehood.

Other major speeches fleshed out the theoretical scope of the Bush Doctrine. At the West Point commencement in June 2002, President Bush argued that new political and technological circumstances threatened to upset the American predominance upon which the post–Cold War peace rested. "The gravest danger to freedom lies at the perilous crossroads of radicalism and technology," he said. "With the spread of chemical, biological and nuclear weapons, along with ballistic missile technology . . . even weak states and small groups could attain a catastrophic power to strike great nations."[43] This was a set of circumstances that demanded a new U.S. military posture:

> For much of the last century, America's defense relied on the Cold War doctrines of deterrence and containment. In some cases, those strategies still apply. But new threats also require new thinking. Deterrence—the promise of massive retaliation against nations—means nothing against shadowy terrorist networks with no nation or citizens to defend. Containment is not possible when unbalanced dictators with weapons of mass destruction can deliver those weapons on missiles or secretly provide them to terrorist allies. We cannot defend America and our friends by hoping for the best. We cannot put our faith in

the word of tyrants, who solemnly sign non-proliferation treaties, and then systematically break them. If we wait for threats to fully materialize, we will have waited too long.[44]

The Bush Doctrine came to full flower three months later, with the release of the formal *National Security Strategy of the United States* (NSS).[45] The NSS originates in the observation that "the United States possesses unprecedented—and unequalled—strength and influence in the world." The Bush administration announced its intention to leverage "the unipolar moment" to exercise "a distinctly American internationalism"—a phrase first used in the Reagan Library speech, given new meaning by a new commitment of American power—"that reflects the union of our values and our national interests. The aim of this strategy is to help make the world not just safer but better."[46]

Driven by moral imperatives, blessed with unprecedented power, the NSS made it the duty of the United States to extend the Pax Americana.

The Road to War

The NSS has proved to be the exception to the Bush administration's policy-by-speechmaking habit. As attention, particularly in Congress, turned toward Iraq, pressure began to mount on the administration to speak directly about its intentions toward the regime of Saddam Hussein. The anniversary of the September 11 attacks provided the president with the opportunity to explain how a war against Iraq would fit into his larger set of strategic goals, first on September 11, 2002, at Ellis Island and then the next day before the United Nations General Assembly.

Quite naturally but with a clear purpose, the president began his Ellis Island address by summoning the memory of the previous year's attacks: "September 11, 2001 will always be a fixed point in the life of America," he said. "The loss of so many lives left us to examine our own. Each of us was reminded that we are here only for a time, and these counted days should be filled with things that last and matter."[47] For Bush, the "mission and moment" that began in the aftermath of 9/11 had not ended in Afghanistan, but continued.

It is perhaps here, also, where the Bush Doctrine parted ways with the Clinton past. Both presidents were animated by the vision of a liberal international order in which the United States played a central role. But Bush called for something like Theodore Roosevelt's idea of "the strenuous life," a conscious striving to achieve large and important things; Clinton, with his emphasis on economic forces and international organizations, acted as though the Pax Americana would expand itself, requiring only modest efforts (particularly militarily), wise guidance, and constant consultation with others, whether democratic or autocratic. Bush's rhetoric also revealed a faith in what Abraham Lincoln might have called "providence." Said the president: "I believe there is a reason that history has matched this nation with time."

> There is a line in our time, and in every time, between those who believe all men are created equal, and those who believe some men and women and children are expendable in the pursuit of power. There is a line in our time, and in every time, between the defenders of human liberty and those who seek to master the minds and souls of others. Our generation has heard history's call, and we will answer it. . . .
>
> This nation has defeated tyrants and liberated death camps, raised this lamp of liberty to every captive land. We have no intention of ignoring or appeasing history's latest gang of fanatics trying to murder their way into power. They are discovering, as others before them, the resolve of a great country and a great democracy. In the ruins of two towers, under a flag unfurled at the Pentagon, at the funerals of the lost, we have made a sacred promise to ourselves and to the world: we will not relent until justice is done and our nation is secure. What our enemies have begun, we will finish.[48]

The speech was more than a moving oration at a solemn moment: It introduced, forcefully, new elements into the policy debate over Iraq and the "war on terrorism." No longer was the president's purpose simply measuring justice for the September 11 attacks or a strategic decision to respond to the threat of rogue regimes and weapons proliferation. The president strove to place this larger war within the broadest sweep of American history, quoting the Declaration of Independence, recalling World War II in his references to "death camps" and "appeasement," and evoking the resolve of Lincoln in the Gettysburg Address—another funeral oration intended not simply to commemorate the dead but to dedicate the nation to a future, unfinished task.

Speaking to the United Nations the next day, the president's emphasis returned to the threat posed by Iraq. Global security, he declared, is "challenged by outlaw groups and regimes that accept no law of morality and have no limit to their violent ambitions." Saddam Hussein's Iraq was a perfect example of this new threat: "In one place—in one regime—we find all these dangers, in their most lethal and aggressive forms, exactly the kind of threat the United Nations was born to confront."[49]

But as he reviewed the history of Iraqi actions since the 1990 invasion of Kuwait, the president expanded the "threat theme" to demonstrate that Saddam's intentions and arsenal were dangerous not only in themselves but also to the authority of the United Nations. "Iraq has answered a decade of UN demands with a decade of defiance," he said. "All the world now faces a test, and the United Nations a difficult and defining moment. Are Security Council resolutions to be honored and enforced, or cast aside without consequence? Will the United Nations serve the purpose of its founding, or will it be irrelevant?"[50]

Bush went on to lay out six tests to measure whether Iraq intended to come into compliance with UN resolutions. Either the Iraqis would accept UN resolutions—"the just demands of peace and security"—or "action will be unavoidable" and the United States would go to war. "The purposes of the United States," said President Bush, "should not be doubted." And even if the regime complied, Saddam could not long remain in control of the country, for "a regime that has lost its legitimacy will also lose its power."[51]

Importantly in an international forum, Bush began to make the larger case for political reform in the Islamic world. "If we meet our responsibilities, if we overcome this danger, we can arrive at a very different future," he said.

> The people of Iraq can shake off their captivity. They can one day join a democratic Afghanistan and a democratic Palestine, inspiring reforms throughout the Muslim world. These nations

can show by their example that honest government, and respect for women, and the great Islamic tradition of learning can triumph in the Middle East and beyond. And we will show that the promise of the United Nations can be fulfilled in our time.[52]

These arguments also had a strong effect on opinion in the United States. After weeks of wrangling, Congress finally voted on a resolution authorizing President Bush to go to war. Senator Joseph Lieberman, a moderate Democrat and the vice-presidential nominee in 2000, asserted:

If Saddam Hussein does not comply, or if the United Nations is not willing to take action to enforce its orders, in my opinion, this is the last chance for Saddam Hussein but also the best chance for the international community to come together to prove that the resolutions of the United Nations mean more and have more weight than the paper on which they are written.[53]

Other prominent Democrats agreed. Senator John Edwards observed that the resolution sent a "clear message to Iraq and the world: America stands united in its determination to eliminate forever the threat of Iraq's weapons of mass destruction." He reviewed the risks of war, but concluded that "the risks of inaction are far greater than the risks of action."[54] In the end, both houses of Congress voted overwhelmingly in favor of the war resolution. A pleased President Bush declared, "America speaks with one voice . . . to the international community and the United Nations Security Council. Saddam Hussein and his outlaw regime pose a grave threat to the region, the world, and the United States. Inaction is not an option."[55]

For a time, this logic appeared to carry the day in the United Nations as well. The Security Council adopted Resolution 1441 on November 8, 2002, calling for the disarmament of Iraq and its compliance with previous UN resolutions. It found Iraq in "material breach of these resolutions," and promised "serious consequences"—war—if it did not quickly come into compliance. The council, however, quickly proved that it preferred debate over weapons inspections to any military action, even when, in December, Iraq failed to comply with the provision of 1441 demanding a full accounting of weapons programs.[56]

As during the 1999 Kosovo crisis, the UN revealed that it inherently favored sovereignty over liberty; perhaps the very structure of the organization—it is, after all, a collection of states—made it unfit to accomplish the purposes the president intended. And as one report of inspectors followed another, and as France led an opposition movement both in the United Nations and in the larger court of world opinion, the main question became one of American "unilateralism." The accelerating deployment of U.S. military forces to the region seemed to underscore Bush's "rush to war."

France in particular seemed to relish its role as counterweight to the United States, with French Foreign Minister Dominique de Villepin the public embodiment of this opposition. "If war is the only way to resolve this problem," he said on January 20, 2003, "we are going down a dead end." France, he vowed in an impressive display of circular logic, would never "associate ourselves with military intervention that is not supported by the international community," although it had done so in Kosovo. Germany agreed. War in Iraq, argued Foreign Minister Joschka Fischer, would "have disastrous consequences for long-term regional stability." Berlin was so set against war that it was willing to ignore Iraq's snubbing of UN resolutions. "Iraq has complied fully with all relevant resolutions and cooperated very closely with the UN team on the ground," Fischer contended. "We think things are moving in the right direction, based on the efforts of the inspection team, and [they] should have all the time which is needed."[57] In sum, the vote on Resolution 1441 proved a misleading measure of international will to confront Saddam Hussein militarily.

Thus, by the 2003 State of the Union address, President Bush found himself on the defensive. To regain the initiative, he again argued that the Iraq crisis was a test of the United Nations and that his patience with diplomacy was limited: "America's purpose is more than to follow a process—it is to achieve a result," he said. "[T]he course of this nation does not depend on the decisions of others. Whatever action is required, whenever action is necessary, I will defend the freedom and security of the American people."

Bush also stressed his commitment to a free Iraq. "Tonight I have a message for the brave and oppressed people of Iraq: your enemy is not surrounding your country—your enemy is ruling your country. The day [Saddam Hussein] and his regime are removed from power will be the day of your liberation." And, as before at crucial moments, the president upped the political ante. Addressing another "message" to the U.S. armed forces, he left little doubt that war was imminent:

> Many of you are assembling in or near the Middle East and some crucial hours may lie ahead. In those hours, the success of our cause will depend on you. Your training has prepared you. Your honor will guide you. . . . Sending Americans into battle is the most profound decision a president can make. The technologies of war have changed; the risks and suffering of war have not. For the brave Americans who bear the risk, no victory is free from sorrow. This nation fights reluctantly, because we know the cost and we dread the days of mourning that always come.[58]

With the die so obviously cast, yet still trapped in a dead-end debate about weapons inspections, the administration sent Secretary of State Colin Powell before the United Nations Security Council to try to preserve the prospect of a wartime coalition of traditional Western allies. Powell's February 5 presentation was a dramatic show of satellite photographs, intercepts of Iraqi military radio communications, and information provided by Iraqi defectors. Not only did Powell make the case that Iraq had not disarmed, but he also suggested that Saddam's links to terrorist organizations were substantial and increasing. "My colleagues," Powell beseeched in summary, "we have an obligation to our citizens, we have an obligation to this body, to see that our resolutions are complied with."[59]

Yet for all its drama, the presentation was an immediate failure. The echoes of Powell's speech had barely died within the UN when other members of the Security Council voiced skepticism. Powell "failed in front of the world to prove that [Saddam] is a threat to the world," declared Jacques Myard, a member of the French parliament. "The U.S. really lost a great opportunity today."[60] For others, evidence of weapons was simply a reason for more intense inspections. Over the following weekend, at the *Wehrkunde* conference in Munich—traditionally an expression of transatlantic and particularly German-American solidarity—Fischer spat angrily at Defense Secretary Donald Rumsfeld, "Excuse me, I'm not convinced!"[61]

In part, the transatlantic divide transcended any debate over Iraqi WMD. For all the postwar hand-wringing over intelligence failures about Saddam's weapons stocks, the Bush administration's determination to remove Saddam Hussein had less to do with his regime's armaments than its character. It was, in the president's reckoning, the despotic nature of the Iraqi regime that was the source of the danger. More than any other country in the region, Saddam Hussein's terror state epitomized the broader political dysfunction responsible for the phenomenon of Islamist terrorism. And as long as Saddam Hussein and his thuggish retinue remained in power, the potential for the democratization and liberalization of the region would be severely restrained.

Iraq, in short, was always about more than weapons. It was about Saddam Hussein and the failure of the United States—for the past sixty years—to confront the political sinkhole created by the tyrants of the Middle East. President Bush's February 28, 2003, speech to the American Enterprise Institute is worth quoting at length in this regard:

> The current Iraqi regime has shown the power and tyranny to spread discord and violence in the Middle East. A liberated Iraq can show the power of freedom to transform that vital region, by bringing hope and progress into the lives of millions. America's interests in security and America's belief in liberty both lead in the same direction: to a free and peaceful Iraq. . . .
>
> There was a time when many said that the cultures of Japan and Germany were incapable of sustaining democratic values. Well, they were wrong. Some say the same of Iraq today. They are mistaken. The nation of Iraq—with its proud heritage, abundant resources and skilled and educated people—is fully capable of moving toward democracy and living in freedom.

The world has an interest in spreading democratic values, because stable and free nations do not breed the ideologies of murder. They encourage the peaceful pursuit of a better life. And there are hopeful signs of a desire for freedom in the Middle East. Arab intellectuals have called on Arab governments to address the "freedom gap" so their peoples can fully share in the progress of our times. Leaders in the region speak of a new Arab character that champions internal reform, greater political participation, economic openness and free trade. And from Morocco to Bahrain and beyond, nations are taking genuine steps toward political reform. A new regime in Iraq would serve as a dramatic and inspiring example of freedom for other nations in the region.

It is presumptuous and insulting to suggest that a whole region of the world—the one-fifth of humanity that is Muslim—is somehow untouched by the most basic aspirations of life. Human cultures can be vastly different. Yet the human heart desires the same good things, everywhere on Earth. In our desire to be safe from brutal and bullying oppression, human beings are the same. In our desire to care for our children and give them a better life, we are the same. For these fundamental reasons, freedom and democracy will always and everywhere have greater appeal than the slogans of hatred and tactics of terror. . . .

Much is asked of America in this year 2003. The work ahead is demanding. It will be difficult to help freedom take hold in a country that has known three decades of dictatorship, secret police, internal divisions and war. It will be difficult to cultivate liberty and peace in the Middle East, after so many generations of strife. Yet, the security of our nation and the hope of millions depend on us, and Americans do not turn away from duties because they are hard. We have met great tests in other times and we will meet the tests of our time.[62]

This is a speech that Bill Clinton, or indeed almost any American president, might have made; it is imbued with liberal political principles that the American Founders would recognize as essentially the same as their own. The first President Bush used this sort of rhetoric to take the United States and the world to war in 1990. "Nothing of this moral importance since World War II has faced the nation," he said of his confrontation with Saddam Hussein.[63] Yet Bush 41 had fought a war with strictly limited objectives. Coming from Bill Clinton's mouth, a paean to human liberty would elaborate what he would regard as very good reasons for avoiding a war. But for George W. Bush, these were fighting words.

On March 17, 2003, President Bush issued a forty-eight-hour ultimatum for the regime of Saddam Hussein to relinquish power and leave Iraq. A failure by Saddam to do so, he said, "will result in military conflict, commenced at a time of our choosing." In his final prewar address, the president pledged to "build a new Iraq that is prosperous and free."

> The United States, with other countries, will work to advance liberty and peace in [the Middle East]. Our goal will not be achieved overnight, but it can come over time. The power and appeal of human liberty is felt in every life and in every land. . . . That is the future we choose. Free nations have a duty to defend our people by uniting against the violent. Tonight, as we have done before, America and our allies accept that responsibility.[64]

Operation Iraqi Freedom began two days later.

PART II

Military Planning

The story of military planning for Operation Iraqi Freedom is largely the story of the discovery of the true meaning of "regime change." What proved to be the larger purpose of the war—the beginning of the political transformation of the Middle East—did not define the military mission.

While much of the world sparred publicly from the summer of 2002 until the spring of 2003 over the question of whether to go to war in Iraq, the Pentagon's defense planners and strategists understood the question somewhat differently. For them, there was no real break in contact between the U.S. and Iraqi militaries since the withdrawal of the large American force assembled for Operation Desert Storm in 1991. From Operation Provide Comfort, intended to protect the Kurds in northern Iraq following their uprising against Saddam after Desert Storm, through the establishment of the "Northern Watch" and "Southern Watch" no-fly zones (which resulted in a greater number of aircraft sorties than Desert Storm and Operation Iraqi Freedom combined—more than 150,000 flights under Operation Southern Watch alone), and punctuated by periodic larger-scale strikes such as 1998's Operation Desert Fox, the American war against Saddam Hussein had already lasted for more than twelve years. Thus, the United States was never confronted with the choice of whether to embrace or refrain from military action against Iraq, but rather, whether to continue a military action designed to contain Saddam Hussein's regime or launch a military action designed to end it.

As most of the U.S. and coalition operations against Saddam Hussein since the end of the Gulf War suggest, the planning during the 1990s for large-scale conventional military contingencies in the Middle East was essentially reactive: a replay of Desert Storm, beginning with the defense of Saudi Arabia and ending with a counterattack to liberate Kuwait—but stopping short of ousting Saddam from power.

During this "interwar" period, the naturally conservative outlook of senior military leaders was exacerbated by the steep reductions in U.S. military strength that began in earnest after Desert Storm. The cuts outlined during the last year of the first Bush administration, directed by then chairman of the Joint Chiefs of Staff Colin Powell's "Base Force" plan, grew deeper by about 20 percent under the Clinton administration's "Bottom-Up Review" of 1993. From more than 900,000 soldiers on active duty during the Gulf War, the army was cut to just over 500,000; air force and navy strength were reduced nearly as much. Only the Marine Corps retained anything approaching its Cold War structure. The weapons modernization program that had produced the overwhelming victory of Desert Storm was subsequently slowed by Bush and further slowed by Clinton; in all, hundreds of billions of dollars in planned procurement were either deferred or cancelled outright.

At the same time, the chaos of the early post–Cold War years steadily increased the pace of global operations demanded of this far smaller force. Not only was the American presence in the Persian Gulf region indefinitely extended, but the bloody collapse of Yugoslavia slowly but inexorably siphoned a share of Pentagon resources as well. Heightened uncertainty in East Asia also troubled Pentagon planners. In 1993 and 1994, North Korea's aggressive behavior made the possibility of war on the peninsula loom large. And in 1995 and 1996, China's provocative actions toward Taiwan, including a so-called "missile blockade" exercise that bracketed the island's ports, demanded an American show of strength in response.

Tacked on to these traditional strategic threats was a growing concern with humanitarian crises and the chaos produced by so-called "failed states." War was averted in Haiti in 1994 when military strongman Raoul Cedras was talked out of power, but only under the threat of invasion by 20,000 U.S. troops from ships anchored offshore. Cedras's replacement by Jean Bertrand Aristide brought little real progress to Haiti and required a long-term UN peacekeeping presence with American participation. Most significant—far beyond the immediate military effect—was the mission to Somalia, begun in 1992 under the first Bush administration and terminated in early 1994 in the aftermath of the disastrous "Black Hawk Down" raid in October 1993. To many in the military and government, Somalia proved the lesson of Vietnam and Lebanon: that American public opinion could not stomach casualties in pursuit of difficult-to-define political objectives.

In short, it would be difficult to conceive an environment less conducive to a reconsideration of U.S. military strategy and war-planning toward Iraq. Not until the late Clinton years—and notably, after the passage by Congress of the Iraq Liberation Act that made "regime change" the formal policy of the United States—did U.S. Central Command look seriously at the challenges of pushing beyond defending Saudi Arabia and Kuwait and begin to replot the "road to Baghdad."

The baseline version of the plan that would evolve into Operation Iraqi Freedom—1003V, or "ten-oh-three-Victor"—was written in 1996. Initially nothing more than deployment rosters or, in Pentagonese, "time-phased force deployment data" (TPFDDs), the plan forecast a force of two U.S. corps-sized formations and more than 1,000 aircraft, with a two-week air-only campaign preceding joint air-land operations. It could be triggered by any significant threat from Iraq and covered contingencies from a deterrent posture to try to forestall an Iraqi move against Kuwait or Saudi Arabia, through a massive buildup lasting ninety days, the defense of Kuwait and Saudi Arabia, and, finally, offensive operations into Iraq, aimed at Baghdad.[1]

Army General Tommy Franks, chief of CENTCOM during Iraqi Freedom, had begun to reshape 1003V during his tenure as commander of U.S. Third Army, the main army component of CENTCOM. Two factors entered into his calculus in reworking the war plan. First, the defense of Kuwait had grown significantly easier during the 1990s. Forward basing and prepositioning had vastly improved U.S. initial combat power in the region, and the Iraqi army had been weakened by sanctions and restricted in its operations by the no-fly and no-drive zones. Thus, although Saddam still presented a potential invasion threat, it was much reduced.

The second factor was the deterioration of U.S.-Saudi relations and military cooperation. The kingdom continued to permit U.S. aircraft to police the skies from Saudi bases, but had several times refused to cooperate during punitive strikes against Saddam. By 1997, it seemed an unlikely assumption that the Saudis would allow the Americans to stage an invasion force from the kingdom. Consequently, Franks and his staff began to focus on other deployment options.

Planning for Iraq after 9/11

Four days after the September 11 attacks, President Bush rallied with his principal lieutenants at Camp David, the presidential retreat in Maryland's Catoctin Mountains. The president had already declared the terrorist strikes to be an act of war, and there was growing consensus that a "war on terrorism" would have to include states that gave aid and comfort to al Qaeda and other terrorist groups of global reach. Clearly, the Taliban regime in Afghanistan fit this description, but so did Syria and Iran. Deputy Defense Secretary Paul Wolfowitz raised the question of Iraq; in fact, the problem of Islamist terrorism was, at its heart, the problem of the dysfunctional political order in the Arab world and the greater Middle East. To most administration principals, how to deal with Afghanistan was enough for the moment—most accounts of the meeting tend to portray Wolfowitz as fixated on Iraq and Saddam Hussein—but the debate between a narrow and broad interpretation of the war on terrorism had begun.[2]

Despite the priority placed upon Afghanistan, initial discussions about Iraq took place well before the defeat of the Taliban was secure. In late November 2001, the president asked Defense Secretary Donald Rumsfeld to investigate the condition of Pentagon war plans against Iraq.[3] The next month, General Franks traveled from Afghanistan to President Bush's ranch in Crawford, Texas, where the president was spending his Christmas and New Year's holidays. While most of the discussion was directed toward the situation in Central Asia, the meeting also provided an opportunity to explain the 1003V plan to the president. Significantly, Rumsfeld was not present. He had been briefed on the war plan in a video conference ten days previously and had suggested that Franks explain it to President Bush.

Through the difficulties of the Afghan campaign, President Bush and General Franks developed a good rapport. In a brief press appearance together on December 28, 2001, Bush voiced his trust in Franks, calling him "precisely the kind of man we need to lead a complex mission such as this."[4]

In his discussions with the president, Franks described the full-blown version of the 1003V plan, what would become known as the "generated start" force—meaning that it would follow the complete deployment plan and get the entire force in place prior to the beginning of any attack. Later, Franks gave his subordinates the clear impression that President Bush seemed at ease with the size of the force and the length of time to deploy required by the plan, although Franks stressed that this was simply the "off-the-shelf" plan and that changes could and would be proposed. At the same time, CENTCOM planners understood that they could not, as one senior general put it, "tip the president's hand, discuss [planning] the coalition, or push Saddam" until public opinion was ready to accept it.

Another outcome of the Crawford meeting was a recognition that Franks could soon be running more than one war. In addition to Iraq, counterterrorism operations were accelerating around the Horn of Africa, and, of course, ongoing in Afghanistan. Unlike General Norman Schwarzkopf during the first Gulf War, Franks would not have the luxury of burying himself too deeply in the tactical minutiae of Iraq; he would have to remain a regional commander-in-chief, translating political and strategic guidance from civilian leaders to subordinate headquarters, who would actually create the plan and, in the event, conduct the operation.

This, in turn, necessitated a change in the way the Bush administration's high command was running Afghanistan. Several months into Operation Enduring Freedom, Franks was still having twice-daily phone conversations with Secretary Rumsfeld, covering the details of current operations: how many patrols were out, what was happening with Special Operations teams, and so forth. Periodically, there would be larger video conferences, Franks with his staff and Rumsfeld with his principal lieutenants—Deputy Secretary Paul Wolfowitz, Undersecretary for Policy Douglas Feith, Undersecretary for Intelligence Steven Cambone, Generals Richard Myers and Peter Pace from the Joint Chiefs of Staff, and others. Whereas CENTCOM commanders were looking for specific guidance, Rumsfeld often had more questions than answers.

Developing a pattern that would come to dominate discussions about Iraq planning—and indeed, Iraq operations to this day—many of these Afghanistan conferences revolved around the number of U.S. troops deployed to the country. Initially the Pentagon capped troop strength at

3,500, fearing that anything larger would "look like an occupation," as one participant characterized the concern. To the CENTCOM generals, the idea seemed to be to employ the minimum amount of force necessary to defeat the Taliban, and not one soldier more. While it had been initially a tremendous challenge simply to project American military power to such a remote spot on the globe, the combination of the Afghan Northern Alliance with U.S. Special Forces, CIA operatives, and precision air power was proving devastatingly successful. Consequently, there had been no need to wait until spring to push southward toward Kabul, Kandahar, and the other Taliban strongholds, as initially considered.

The war was, if anything, moving faster than Franks desired. Relations with the Northern Alliance became strained, most prominently at the battle of Tora Bora where cooperation between the U.S. force and its Afghan allies collapsed and probably allowed Osama bin Laden to escape the trap that Franks had laid for him.

Gradually, the size of the U.S. force crept up—first to 5,000, then to 7,000. Still, the premise was that this would be a temporary expedient followed by a rapid drawdown once a new Afghan government and army were in place, or after the International Security Assistance Force (ISAF) "internationalized" the mission. But deploying and sustaining ISAF quickly proved problematic—reflected in the troubles of the German Bundeswehr, which had to rely on unreliable Ukrainian airlift and could barely maintain a rotational force of 1,000. At the same time, elements of al Qaeda and the Taliban began a low-level insurgency in the Pashtun-majority regions in southern and eastern Afghanistan. As a result, U.S. force levels kept escalating. By mid-2002, more than 10,000 American soldiers were in Afghanistan, and approximately that number remain there today.

The Afghanistan experience also revealed the weakness and imprecision of the Pentagon's deployment methods. The marine expeditionary units that moved into southern Afghanistan simply took all the equipment and troops they could muster for the mission, all but ignoring the limits on personnel numbers. And the army's standard deployment procedures often did not capture Franks's intent. In one case, Franks approved the deployment of a company of military police to guard the American headquarters compound, expecting that this would be a fairly simple matter of putting several hundred soldiers and their personal gear on a plane; the army instead prepared to ship

the unit's High Mobility Multipurpose Wheeled Vehicles and other equipment as well, a move that would require many more airlift sorties. The
service—and the traditional TPFDD process—normally deployed units
according to their table of organization and equipment, and, absent specific
instructions to the contrary, did not have a good method for tracking anything
different. This system would prove even more troublesome in the months to
come, as deployment plans for Iraq were readied.

The surprisingly quick victory in Afghanistan—or what was perceived as a victory—also shaped the war-plan debate within the Office of
the Secretary of Defense. The initially successful cooperation between
U.S. and local Afghan forces revived for a time the notion of combining
American strike power with local Iraqi opposition such as the Kurdish
peshmerga guerrillas and exile groups allied under the Iraqi National
Congress. Although these sorts of schemes do not appear to have formed
a very serious element in formal campaign planning, they did reinforce
the idea—also touted by airpower advocates and those arguing for the
"transformation" of the U.S. military—that victory in Iraq would require
far less force than had Operation Desert Storm.

This perception persisted even though the military objective—"regime
change"—was now far more ambitious than ejecting the Iraqi army from
Kuwait or destroying the Republican Guard's capacity as an invasion force.
Indeed, the simplistic understanding of regime change nurtured by many in
the Pentagon defined the physical conquest of Baghdad as the strategic "center of gravity." If Saddam and his immediate lieutenants were decapitated
from the body of Iraqi society, it was assumed, the government and rest of
society would continue to function. The "regime" was thus perceived as
inherently brittle, its violent and corrupt ways having alienated it from the
majority of Iraqis who, once convinced that Saddam was gone, would rally in
support of their American liberators. In this reading, it would be possible to
topple Ba'athism with a single, sharp blow, were it delivered with enough
speed, precision, and strength.

Of course, other strategic objectives competed with "regime change,"
such as the seizure of Saddam's WMD. This was understood to be an
imprecise science at best, however, as the Iraqis were believed to have
effectively dispersed the components of their doomsday complex in order
to conceal it from UN weapons inspectors.

A second objective was to prevent Saddam from attacking Israel, as he had done in 1991, and thus widen the war into a regional conflagration. While inspections had accounted for a large number of Scud-type missiles, the possibility that Saddam had stashed away a small number of these munitions or developed an alternate means of delivery could not be discounted; even assuming military operations were more successful than the frustrating "Scud hunt" in Operation Desert Storm, this sort of preventive action would demand significant forces and intense effort.

Other considerations included a variety of spoiling actions Iraqi forces might take, such as setting fire to oil wells as they had done during the Iraqi retreat from Kuwait in 1991. Military planners were also concerned that Saddam might sabotage critical infrastructure, by dynamiting dams to slow the advance of U.S. forces, or turn against his own population—releasing chemical or biological agents against the Kurds or Shi'a.

Deep differences of opinion and practice marked the many personalities and institutions shaping the plan for Operation Iraqi Freedom. There was, of course, the rivalry between Rumsfeld's Pentagon, Powell's State Department, and George Tenet's Central Intelligence Agency. But Pentagon policymakers also distrusted the caution of many senior military officers, who, it was felt, were entrenched against Rumsfeld's reform agenda and leery of deeper involvement in the Middle East. There were also widely differing viewpoints among the services. But probably the largest gap of all lay between the two parties who would ultimately be most responsible for shaping and executing the war plan: Secretary Rumsfeld and the U.S. Army.

Rumsfeld viewed the army as a hidebound and headstrong institution unwilling or unable to accept the realities of modern war implicit in his vision of transformation, which emphasized speed and agility. As early as the spring of 2001, after the new secretary of defense made clear his intention to target the army's Crusader artillery system and two of the army's ten divisions, Rumsfeld's relationship with Army Chief of Staff General Eric Shinseki became famously heated. Rumsfeld's choice for Shinseki's replacement was leaked fourteen months before his term was officially up, essentially making Shinseki a lame duck through his last year of service.

The bureaucratic fight soon exploded into full view on Capitol Hill, with the army lobbying on behalf of the Crusader and, in a none-too-subtle subtext, against Rumsfeld's vision for transformation. "A decision to kill Crusader puts soldiers at risk," a memorandum of talking points explained, warning that Rumsfeld's program risked a return to the "hollow army" of the 1970s. The Defense Department, in turn, seized the memorandum as a case of rank insubordination against civilian authority and ordered an investigation by the Army's Inspector General. *Armed Forces Journal International* thus neatly captured the mood in the Pentagon during the run-up to the war with Iraq, when it published in the summer of 2002 a cover featuring a picture of Secretary Rumsfeld and the headline, "Does He Really Hate the Army?"

At the heart of the war-planning debate were contending imperatives. On the one hand was the need for a rapid deployment—the need to preserve President Bush's options without seeming to commit the administration to war militarily before the political decision had been made. On the other hand, however, was the need to deploy sufficient force both to win the war and establish the security necessary for reconstruction. Throughout months of planning, these competing impulses were never completely harmonized, the inherent tensions never resolved.

A central issue was the willingness and ability of the Iraqi army to resist. Assessing the state of the Iraqi military was, despite the experience of Desert Storm and ongoing operations since, a tricky business. The intangible factors that ultimately determine the strength of any military organization—the quality of its leadership, troop morale, the state of force readiness, and training—were virtually impossible to measure from outside. Iraqi military and political leaders had for decades learned how to lie to one another, simply to survive in Saddam's paranoid regime. Further, U.S. intelligence-gathering efforts focused intensively on issues of most immediate concern, such as threats to aircraft in no-fly zones and Iraqi WMD programs. Strategic-level assessments were indistinguishable from U.S. policy judgments. When American political leaders looked at Iraq, they saw what they wanted to see.

There were, however, some realities that were too large to miss. As a field force, the Iraqi army never recovered from Desert Storm. While it was sufficiently strong to put down the postwar uprisings in the Kurdish north and the Shi'a south, and, absent American attention, still posed an invasion threat to Kuwait, any larger operation was well beyond its capability. Iraq's tank fleet was down to approximately 40 percent of its previous size and the number of infantry fighting vehicles had been reduced even further—from nearly 7,000 to less than 2,000. Self-propelled artillery, the system most suitable for delivering chemical rounds, was down to approximately 150 howitzers and rocket-launchers. The overall strength of the Iraqi army was perhaps 350,000 to 400,000 soldiers. For all practical purposes, the Iraqi air force was no factor; it did not muster a single sortie during Operation Iraqi Freedom.[5]

More important than the formal order of battle, the Iraqi army had conducted little if any meaningful, realistic, large-scale training or operations—other than repressing its own populace—for more than a decade, with the possible exception of its maneuvers in 1994. Much of the Iraqi army remained organized under four regional headquarters, and even the Republican Guard forces rarely ventured far from their barracks. Even within the Guard and among the more competent units of the regular army, Iraqi ground forces were disposed in a "piecemeal" fashion, by brigades rather than in divisions or corps. To pose a serious, large-scale threat to any coalition attack, the Iraqi army would have to come out of its garrisons, mass, and maneuver. It was initially unprepared to stand and fight as it had done during the tank battles of Desert Storm. Judging by its formations, it appeared that the Iraqi army's first purpose was to try to survive U.S. air attacks.

Most important of all were the state of Iraqi morale and the reliability of its subordinate commanders. American officers and analysts believed that while the average Iraqi foot soldier might have little stomach for a toe-to-toe fight with American forces, the core of the Republican Guard—which was regarded as the primary military obstacle in Iraq—would essentially repeat its Desert Storm performance. That is, it had little ability to inflict serious losses or to conduct large-scale maneuvers while under air attack, but it would attempt local counterattacks and generally stand and fight, if not for the sake of Saddam's regime, then out of nationalism and some sense of professional pride.

The Need for Speed

Yet, in a paradoxical but true sense, much of American campaign planning paid little heed to Iraqi tactical capabilities. Again, the discussions in the Pentagon, CENTCOM, and elsewhere were largely debates about how small a force would be needed to achieve U.S. goals and how quickly American superiority could be exploited to topple the regime.

Indeed, rapid deployment was so much the first order of business that an initial ground option, evolving out of the late 2001 "Vigilant Warrior" war games of the Army's V Corps—the annual command-post exercises of the lone large ground force remaining in Europe and eventually the headquarters that conducted the principal land attack of Iraqi Freedom—called for establishing a toehold in southern Iraq while the full force prescribed by the 1003V plan was readied for the march to Baghdad.

This small ground force—the one armored brigade of the First Cavalry Division then training in Kuwait; the Third Armored Cavalry Regiment engaged in the traditional "Bright Star" exercises in Egypt; the marine expeditionary unit constantly on rotation in the Gulf; plus part of the 101st Airborne Division from Fort Campbell, Kentucky, and the Apache helicopters of the 11th Attack Helicopter Regiment, based in Germany; and a few other V Corps assets—would push into Iraq far enough to protect against missile attacks while the rest of the force deployed through Kuwait. An even faster but still more limited version of this plan, known as "Contingency Plan Wood," would use the forces already in theater to seize Iraq's southern oil fields. The 101st Airborne was to secure the key crossing site on the Euphrates River at the Iraqi town of Nasiriyah. The five- to seven-division force described in the 1003V plan would take as many as 120 days to deploy and prepare for a further attack aimed at Baghdad. Even assembling a ground invasion force of that size would be difficult for a smaller army, more dispersed by peacekeeping and other contingency missions; a good part of V Corps itself was employed in "stabilization" missions to Bosnia and Kosovo. In addition, the plan did not deal with Iraqi forces north of Baghdad—indeed, what to do about northern Iraq remained a planning challenge and, in the event, an operational and strategic challenge as well.

As the initial Afghanistan campaign wound to its conclusion in the spring of 2002, detailed planning for an invasion of Iraq accelerated. As before, V Corps was the primary planning headquarters. This odd arrangement—the V Corps' headquarters in Heidelburg, Germany, is an ocean away from the CENTCOM headquarters in Tampa, Florida, and the Corps normally reported to U.S. European Command—was more necessity than choice. But the army's most "expeditionary" command, XVIII Airborne Corps at Fort Bragg, North Carolina, was now providing the headquarters for the Afghanistan joint task force. III Corps, from Fort Hood, Texas, had been most recently oriented on

Korean contingencies, as had the skeleton I Corps from Fort Lewis, Washington. Not only was the army hard-pressed to provide the necessary command structure for a large operation in Iraq—and unlike Desert Storm, when General Norman Schwarzkopf had run the land campaign, there would also be a three-star "land forces component command," coordinating the maneuvers of the army, marines, and whatever coalition forces were to participate in the invasion. Further, the situation made it impossible to maintain the traditional, habitual relationships between higher headquarters and lower units, and the trust and familiarity that often eased planning and increased understanding of commanders' intent. Operation Iraqi Freedom would be fought largely by forces, staffs, and commanders who had not previously worked together and who, in some cases, shared differing views of operations.

At this point, "regime removal," not "regime change," was the unquestioned purpose of the campaign. The distinction may seem semantic, but it reflected a crucial distinction about basic understanding of the purpose of the war and the limits of military operations. "Regime removal" suggested that removing Saddam Hussein and his lieutenants from power was a sufficient goal; "regime change" implied that, while it was necessary to remove Saddam, it was also mandatory to replace the regime with something better—and, vitally, to provide sufficient occupation forces available to secure what might be a long period of transition. The desire to limit the military ends and thereby limit the military means is vitally important to understanding not only the major combat of Operation Iraqi Freedom, but also the instability and insurgency that have followed.

From April through July 2002, V Corps conducted an exercise it called "Decisive Victory," employing the full "generated start" force in a two-corps, three-pronged, simultaneous assault to isolate Baghdad. Beginning from a narrow front in Kuwait, V Corps and the First Marine Expeditionary Force would drive northward, with the marines securing Iraq's southern oil fields and positioning themselves for further operations. Seizing the bridges at Nasiriyah was the key to these follow-on maneuvers, with the marines intended to attack up the Tigris River valley, while V Corps moved with an armored division on each side of the Euphrates River.

After securing the river crossing, the second phase would be an attack to a line about 150 miles from Baghdad. A number of factors worked against an all-out dash to the capital. The first was a desire to coordinate the attack on the city itself. Baghdad was a sprawling megalopolis of five million residents. Despite its many broad avenues—the sort of stage Saddam loved for military spectacles, parades, and rallies—fighting in an urban environment was inherently risky, mitigating many of the technological advantages enjoyed by U.S. forces. The first task would be to isolate the city by setting up the same sort of loose cordon envisaged in the "Road to Baghdad" plan of 1991.

A second question was the sheer length of the line of communication and supply from Kuwait into Iraq. This was potentially a tremendous vulnerability. A staff study revealed nearly 170 "sensitive sites"—points that might require a squad of infantry to defend. At some point before entering the Baghdad area, there would need to be an operational pause to allow for refueling, rearming, and to allow weary troops and commanders some rest. It was vitally important that the attack not lose momentum before Baghdad was isolated; this was a special concern in the region around the town of Karbala and in the so-called "Karbala Gap," a narrow strip of flat land at the south end of Lake Razaza and running northeast toward Baghdad from an escarpment above the Euphrates River plain.

A third question was how to deal with northern Iraq, where there were both Iraqi forces and oil fields. Moreover, the "Sunni heartland" north of Baghdad up to Tikrit and Mosul contained the elements of Iraqi society most supportive of Saddam's regime, which would need to be pacified. Also in the north were the Kurds, who had established de facto autonomy under an American security umbrella. Although Kurdish leaders insisted that they would not seek their own independent state in the aftermath of an American invasion, Turkey—which had long fought a bloody civil war with its own secessionist Kurds—feared that removing Saddam Hussein would precipitate precisely that.

Thus there were strong military and political arguments in favor of creating a "northern front," not only to put greater pressure on Iraq but also to prevent the Turks and Kurds from fighting each other. General Franks was particularly attracted to the idea of a northern attack, as were British commanders and planners when, early in 2002, they began to be drawn into the planning process.

Deploying through ports in Turkey and sustaining another long line of supply and communication into northern Iraq posed tremendous logistical problems, especially for the United Kingdom. Nevertheless, the British military would play a profound role in the planning and execution of Operation Iraqi Freedom. That the British had taken the lessons of September 11 to heart became apparent in July 2002, when British Secretary of State for Defence Geoffrey Hoon released an update of basic British strategy, entitled "A New Chapter." The white paper reflected profound changes in British strategic thinking, albeit many of them not fully accepted by much of Prime Minister Tony Blair's own Labour Party.

In contrast to Franco-German attitudes, the white paper acknowledged— and indeed, embraced—U.S. global leadership and argued for solidifying the traditional "special relationship" between America and Great Britain as the bulwark of a new coalition designed to prosecute the global war on terrorism. As Minister Hoon put it in his introduction, "September 11 and its aftermath underlined the importance of the transatlantic relationship. From the outset, we demonstrated by our actions our wish to work closely with our most important ally, the United States. Our ability to operate alongside the United States (and with other partners, particularly in Europe but also elsewhere) will be key to future success."[6]

The point of British departure from other major European nations was to take seriously the need to deploy large-scale and effective forces "out of area," particularly to the Middle East. As the white paper put it, "It is likely that, if anything, the trend towards expeditionary operations . . . will become more pronounced." Moreover, it accepted that "a coherent and effective campaign against terrorism . . . may require engagement further afield more often than perhaps we had previously anticipated."[7]

Reprising the policy of the Thatcher government at the time of Operation Desert Storm, Blair and his senior military officials were keen on playing a major role in the invasion of Iraq, a sentiment that led them to offer to lead the attack through Turkey and—a very important factor for a thinly stretched U.S. Army—to provide a corps-level headquarters for the maneuver.

Beyond the ground campaign, there was the question of how air power would be brought to bear to remove Saddam from power. In 1991, the Desert Storm air campaign had begun a full thirty-eight days before the one hundred–hour land war. Coalition air power had pounded frontline Iraqi units, targets in Baghdad, and, to some degree, the Republican Guard heavy forces that were the second line of the Iraqi defenses in Kuwait. Although it did not dislodge Saddam from control of his country, many air power advocates believed that the air war was the militarily decisive factor in the Gulf War campaign.

Subsequent experience in the Balkans reinforced this belief. President Clinton refused to employ U.S. ground forces to drive Serbian troops out of Kosovo and—though it required seventy-eight days of incremental, even feckless bombing—Slobodan Milosevic in the end relented. Despite declining defense budgets, the air force and navy had, finally, invested in building larger stocks of precision-guided munitions. These, in turn, had gotten more accurate and less expensive. A significant breakthrough was achieved with the fielding of the Joint Direct Attack Munition (JDAM). The JDAM was actually a guidance kit that received signals from global positioning system satellites and could be fitted on existing "dumb" bombs, thus reducing the price of precision to mere tens of thousands of dollars. The JDAM also did not require a pilot to maintain a laser spotting device on a target, greatly increasing the survivability of the plane dropping the bomb.

These weapons first came into extensive use during the Afghanistan campaign. Even ancient B-52 bombers had been fitted to drop the JDAM, allowing them to fly in direct and accurate support of ground maneuvers, and permitting Special Forces teams to bring tremendous firepower to bear on Taliban positions. Added to the mix of Tomahawk cruise missiles and other precision-guided munitions, the JDAM would make an air war against Iraq even more effective. Moreover, through a decade of no-fly-zone operations, CENTCOM had developed a detailed knowledge of Iraqi military targets—more than 4,000 in all—and the disposition of Iraqi army units. "We knew their asses inside and out," said one senior planner.

Even as the war plan for Iraq matured, it became increasingly clear to V Corps commanders and staff that they were unlikely to be granted sufficient time to deploy the full force. As the summer of 2002 passed, the domestic and international political situation was growing more complicated, as was the guidance from the Pentagon. Instead of a "generated start" that led to full deployment of five to seven divisions before an invasion—a force that was deemed by senior defense officials to be "too big" and a deployment that would take "too long"—planning began for a so-called "running start." This would allow for a shorter time between the beginning of deployment and the initiation of the attack on Iraq—a political imperative that was growing stronger in Washington.

Nevertheless, the capacity to make a quick decision to go to war, deploy rapidly, and then win quickly and decisively was constrained by a variety of military realities. Deployment could not occur without first securing overflight, staging, and basing rights. Neither could a large-scale air campaign. To keep the ground maneuver force small, yet provide it with sufficient firepower by way of air support from tactical-range aircraft—even with a surge in tanker support aircraft—was a challenge, particularly as the ground attack proceeded farther from Kuwait toward Baghdad. Close air support would have to fly from inside Iraq itself in order to be on-call for ground forces as they engaged resisting Iraqis. Simply providing sufficient fuel for an expanded air fleet—perhaps as many as 1,000 aircraft—or, for that matter, finding sufficient space to park the planes, would require the construction of pipelines from Kuwaiti refineries to airfields closer to the theater. Planners even considered running a pipeline from Kuwait to the Tallil airfield in southern Iraq.

Eventually, the distinction between deployment and war began to evaporate entirely in the planners' minds. What emerged instead was a shifting set of options, dubbed "blue," "white," and "red," distinguished simply by the amount of time needed to prepare for combat. The "blue" option, essentially a large air strike and limited ground attack based on the forces actually in the Gulf, could be executed in five days; "white" required eleven days; and "red," sixteen days. At some point, there would be a sufficient ground force—at least three division equivalents—to initiate the full-scale invasion. Deployments would continue even after that point.

Yet all of these options created problems. The army, as part of its post-Vietnam reforms, had shifted much of its logistics support to the Army Reserve and National Guard. It was almost impossible to go to war without mobilizing them. For example, most of the army's bridging units—essential if retreating Iraqis destroyed the overpasses across the Euphrates and, closer to Baghdad, the Tigris rivers—were vested in the reserves. This proved particularly irksome to Rumsfeld, who understandably wanted to build an invasion force without signaling a clear intent to go to war while international diplomacy was still unfolding. But that was precisely what former army chief of staff Creighton Abrams and the officers of the Vietnam generation had designed the system to prevent. Linking the active and reserve components was intended to force political leaders to make decisions about war—to limit their options—so that the service would not be required to fight a war without the support of the American public.

A smaller force also limited ground planners' options. Through the summer of 2002, V Corps considered how to attack with a single corps while a second corps deployed. Another limiting factor was the difficulty of deployment using only the ports in Kuwait; the Desert Storm deployment, by contrast, had enjoyed the luxury of using the huge, modern facilities in Saudi Arabia, but the Saudis, it was assumed, would not be participating in any campaign to overthrow another Arab government. While the Kuwaitis proved remarkably cooperative, allowing U.S. and British forces to use more than half their commercial piers, there was no way to avoid a natural bottleneck in their limited infrastructure. Support and logistics capabilities—needed to sustain operations deep into Iraq—would be the deployment "billpayers" for combat units. Bridging and truck companies, military police, fuel handling and hauling equipment, civil affairs, and psychological operations units were often pushed lower down the deployment schedule than normally acceptable to army doctrine.

The shortage of support troops also limited attack options toward Baghdad. Army Lieutenant General David D. McKiernan, coalition commander of the land component of the invasion force, wanted to attack Baghdad on multiple fronts, or "axes of approach." The marines would take the easternmost route, and the main army thrust would remain west of the Euphrates until it reached the vicinity of Karbala. But McKiernan also wanted a third axis of approach in the middle, between the Tigris and Euphrates. Even a modest attack would at least mask the larger efforts; Iraqi commanders would have to cover this central approach if for no other reason than it was the shortest and most direct route to Baghdad, with a main highway that ran straight at the heart of the city. Yet V Corps would not have sufficient logistics units to support this second army attack, nor could it afford to secure a second line of supply and communications.

Assembling coherent TPFDDs was also next to impossible in such uncertainty. In all, planning for Operation Iraqi Freedom required seven full-scale deployment conferences, in which all the service components, CENTCOM, and representatives from the Joint Staff and the Office of the Secretary of Defense tried to agree upon a troop movement scheme. Deployment was often the central topic of discussion at the periodic videoconferences between CENTCOM and the Pentagon civilian leadership. Eventually, an entirely new concept of "force packages" was developed, which was, in the words of one participant, a "Chinese menu" approach to deployment—the imperative was, as always, to limit the size of the force, to keep as small a "footprint" as possible.

Yet curiously, most of this debate was about the force necessary to seize Baghdad; there seemed to be far less fuss about the supporting marine attack, the supporting maneuver through Turkey into northern Iraq, or the air campaign. The Pentagon thus reserved the most parsimonious attitude for the one element of the plan that had to succeed in order to remove Saddam Hussein from power.

Nor was there much discussion about what might happen after the fall of Baghdad. Pressed by Democrats while testifying before the Senate Armed Services Committee on February 25, 2003, General Shinseki, then army chief of staff, said that postwar stability operations might require "several hundred thousand soldiers."[8] Two days later, Deputy Secretary Wolfowitz bluntly contradicted this estimate, calling it "way off the mark."[9] The episode highlighted the tensions within the Pentagon over the war plan as well as the extent to which, less than a month before the invasion commenced, there was still no clear understanding of how the military should prepare for what came after Saddam.

"Go Early, Go Ugly"

As Iraq rejected the provisions of UN Resolution 1441 and the prospect of war loomed larger, the planning process accelerated. On December 8, 2002, V Corps completed drafting its "Cobra II" plan of attack, a "rolling start" scheme that broke army deployment into four "force packages." The first of these was premised on rounding out the elements of the Third Infantry Division, based at Fort Stewart, Georgia, that had taken over the rotation for training in Kuwait. That would require about thirty-five days from an alert order. Next in the force flow came the 101st Airborne, beginning with the division headquarters, its fleet of Apache attack and Black Hawk assault helicopters, and one brigade of infantry. Following close behind would be a second brigade of infantry. In all, that deployment would require another thirty-five days. Next in line was the Third Armored Cavalry Regiment, the lone remaining heavy cavalry regiment in the army. Its mix of tanks, fighting vehicles, aircraft, and artillery made it a formidable fighting force, designed to operate independently and over great distances. It might require another forty days to move the regiment and its gear. At that point, 120 days from the beginning of deployment, the First Armored Division from Germany and the First Cavalry Division from Fort Hood, Texas, could be deployed, if needed.

Complicating the army deployment plan was the need to build up the First Marine Expeditionary Force, which eventually totaled more than 80,000 troops (reinforced), and the British First Armoured Division, in reality a mix of an armored brigade, a marine brigade, and an air assault brigade, about 26,000 troops in all. British participation was key, both from a political and operational standpoint, but the plan to have the British lead the attack in the north had run afoul of Turkish objections. Now the British were to come in through the south, operate with the American marines in seizing the port of Umm Qasr, and then take Basra, the second-largest city in Iraq, with a majority Shi'a population and strong anti-Saddam sentiment. In addition, a large proportion of the air force's transport fleet was occupied with moving supplies and munitions for the air campaign. This did not slow the deployment of the ground force—equipment would come by ship, and soldiers, on chartered commercial aircraft—but it did further contribute to congested airfields in Kuwait.

The attack into northern Iraq would now fall to the Army's Fourth Infantry Division, also stationed at Fort Hood, Texas. In strict military terms, this made a great deal of sense; the division was the most modern in the army—its M1 tanks, Bradley fighting vehicles, howitzers, and headquarters all "digitized" with advanced information systems that allowed it to maneuver more rapidly and over extended distances while maintaining communications and command. Again, the challenges of deployment in the north were huge: The force would land at the Turkish port of Iskenderun, then move along a single highway more than 400 miles to the Iraqi border. The thrust into northern Iraq would begin in friendly Kurdish territory, but the region was mountainous—hardly ideal tank country. And once the division made it to central Iraq, it would be attacking toward the city of Mosul and the Sunni heartland, where

Saddam's support was strongest. It was a tough mission, and it had to be carefully coordinated with the attacks from the south.

The deployment plan for the "Cobra II" force was worked out on December 20, 2002—at the sixth of the deployment conferences—and then wargamed by senior commanders and staff a week later at the army's training complex at Grafenwoehr, Germany. Yet even as the final details of the ground scheme of maneuver were being worked out, Rumsfeld and senior defense officials were making deployment decisions at odds with the plan. Rather than agreeing on an attack force of a particular size and composition and building a deployment scheme that most efficiently moved the force to Kuwait, Pentagon leaders and CENTCOM chief General Franks agreed to deploy the force piecemeal, by force packages. In other words, rather than initiating the flow of forces to the Gulf and continuing until complete, the idea was to send one unit or set of units—whatever was defined as a "force package"—then the next increment, and so on. This deployment structure would give the administration maximum latitude for diplomacy: to escalate the threat against Saddam, but preserve the ability to halt the deployment at any stage, with a coherent force in theater. General Franks described the concept as a "highway with off-ramps."

The overall effect was not simply to change the traditional scheme of deployment but to slow it, as became clear at the final deployment conference on January 8, 2003. A secondary effect was to heighten the tension between Rumsfeld and General Shinseki, who was pressing the administration to make timely deployment decisions. Because of the challenges posed by an attack through Turkey, Shinseki wanted to get the Fourth Infantry Division's equipment on ships as soon as possible; he also felt that the main attack toward Baghdad required all of the Third Infantry Division, the 101st Airborne, and the Third Armored Cavalry Regiment. Moreover, there were disagreements about whether the divisions should be deployed with their habitual "slice" of corps support troops. In fact, army divisions were not really self-contained units, but intended to operate within a corps structure, with the corps providing a variety of combat support and combat service support assets, from additional artillery to logistics. The logistics support would be especially essential as the attack progressed toward Baghdad. The 101st Airborne, for example, had its own "101st Corps Support Group," stationed also at Fort Campbell, Kentucky; the support group was, for all practical purposes, part of the division. But under the new deployment plan, the support group was treated as extra, unnecessary baggage and pushed farther down the deployment timeline.

The back-and-forth tradeoffs between deployment and the attack plan resulted in a second version of the "Cobra II" plan, briefed to commanders at the V Corps "Victory Scrimmage" exercises on January 29, again at Grafenwoehr. The reduced force meant that the attack on Baghdad would proceed on just two axes, the army west of the Euphrates and the marines east along the Tigris. The third, "center option," was out.

But in some sense, the planning process was becoming academic, with "Victory Scrimmage" overtaken by events. As the diplomatic process at the United Nations began to fail, war became nearly certain. Franks's new guidance was that the attack would probably have to "go ugly and go early." The air campaign might begin as soon as February 15. At this point, it was simply a scramble to deploy as much force as fast as possible.

Once again, the V Corps planners returned to their maps. But in addition to preparing for a large-scale invasion, they also had a requirement to be able to exploit a "catastrophic success"—the quick collapse of Saddam's regime, either because the Iraqi army refused to fight or because subordinate commanders or Ba'ath party officials decided to oust Saddam themselves. Under such circumstances, it might be necessary to get a U.S. ground force into Baghdad immediately, if only to receive the Iraqi surrender. Thus, a brigade of the Eighty-second Airborne and the division headquarters was added to the deployment plan, to be able to parachute or land at the Baghdad airport in the event of a coup.

Further, the Turkish government's refusal to allow U.S. forces to deploy in preparation for the attack from the north was fast becoming an insoluble problem. Although deployment orders had been issued to the Fourth Infantry Division, and ships laden with its equipment were queued up at Iskenderun, the situation had passed the point of no return; the war would begin—and might well end—before the Fourth Infantry Division could attack. At the same time, the Turks were threatening to push deep into Iraqi Kurdistan, almost certainly provoking a Kurdish response. Although there were U.S. Special Forces already operating in Kurdish-controlled northern Iraq, they were intended to coordinate attacks against Iraqi targets with U.S. air power and Kurdish *peshmerga*—

not mediate a dispute between the Turks and the Kurds. Thus it was decided to insert the Army's 173rd Airborne Regiment—paratroopers stationed in Italy—into northern Iraq once the war began.

What seemed to be the final piece of the puzzle was planning for operations inside Baghdad itself. The objective of "regime removal" demanded that the coalition not simply cordon off the capital but control it. Staff officers had spent months combing all the intelligence they could acquire on Baghdad's infrastructure: its power grid, its sewers—as well as where key people in the Iraqi regime lived and Saddam's most loyal units were garrisoned. A special study was done to understand how the city functioned as a system—how the physical and political infrastructures intertwined—and where its points of vulnerability lay. Before any large conventional force would enter Baghdad, Special Forces and CIA teams would already be at work.

Coordinating army, marine, and air force operations in Baghdad would also be challenging. If all went according to plan, marine and army units would converge on the city and set up a cordon of blocking points on the major routes in and out of Baghdad. The prospect of urban combat—with the echoes of Somalia—was often stressed in the media. And past experience, such as in Operation Just Cause in Panama in 1989, suggested that when a despotic regime finally collapsed, keeping public order and safety would prove difficult. Even the most rapid and successful invasion might falter, or create bloody television images, if Iraqi diehards made a last stand inside Baghdad.

Yet in the final weeks before the war, military commanders remained overwhelmingly occupied with the mad dash of deployment. Major General David Petraeus, commander of the 101st Airborne, had flown the division's helicopters to the port of Jacksonville, Florida, conducting a massive "air assault" rather than shipping the aircraft by train. It was a matter of doing anything to save time. The division also purchased approximately 4,000 commercial airline tickets to Kuwait to build up infantry strength as fast as possible. Just days before the war began, General Franks formally abandoned any pretense of getting the Fourth Infantry Division in through Turkey, rerouting its equipment from the Mediterranean through the Suez Canal to the Red Sea, the Gulf, and ports in Kuwait; his most capable force would not be available to fight until early April, at best.[10]

By mid-March, the final gasps of diplomacy aimed at preventing war were failing. Franks asked his land component commander, Lieutenant General McKiernan, if he had enough troops to invade Iraq and reach Baghdad successfully. "Just enough," replied McKiernan. On March 16, 2003, the coalition force—American and British, with small contingents from Australia and Poland—moved from its assembly areas to its attack positions, cutting lanes in the sand berm that marked the official border between Kuwait and Iraq.

PART III

Major Combat Operations

Against the background of decades of uncertain policymaking and hasty and halting planning, the success of coalition combat operations in Iraq was stunning. The month-long campaign to remove Saddam Hussein's regime from power in Baghdad, despite sometimes desperate moments, was a remarkable feat of arms. And despite the inadequacies of planning for postcombat stability operations, the rapidity of the initial invasion did much to set the conditions for a more complete victory.

The first part of Operation Iraqi Freedom, which President Bush declared complete and victorious May 1, 2003, was a classic, conventional-force invasion, bypassing much of the Iraqi army and culminating with the capture of the enemy capital city, Baghdad. It was preceded by an attempt to "decapitate" Saddam's government and kill him.

On Wednesday, March 19, 2003, the CIA received what it believed was credible intelligence that Saddam Hussein and his sons, Uday and Qusay, would be spending the night in a complex of buildings in southern Baghdad. Although the intelligence was inherently uncertain, a successful strike that either killed or incapacitated Saddam might cause the immediate collapse of Iraqi resistance—the "catastrophic success" that had recently become a part of U.S. military planning. But what made the decision to go after Saddam especially difficult was the fact that it could interfere with the highly choreographed initial plan of attack.[1]

Indeed, more than thirty special operations teams were already in Iraq, executing missions linked to the planned "shock and awe" large-scale air attack. Special Forces teams had forty-eight hours to position themselves before the air campaign began; the major land attack would begin at dawn on March 22. President Bush had a choice to make between snatching the chance to get Saddam and rewriting a finely

52

orchestrated war plan—a plan that had already begun to be executed. In a three-hour meeting to sort through the situation, the president approved a quick strike on the Baghdad complex, in a mission that would probably lose the cover of darkness, involving two F-117A "Stealth" fighter-bombers carrying 2,000 bombs, to be followed up by an attack by Tomahawk cruise missiles. Late in the evening, President Bush went on television to announce the beginning of the war.[2]

In response to the president's decision, Franks asked to advance the timing of the ground attack by a day, while the large-scale air campaign would proceed more or less as planned, to be carried out over several days and involving approximately 3,000 targets. Twenty-four targets were removed from the targeting plan, some because of high risk of collateral damage, but some to permit communication among senior leaders to "allow" the Saddam regime to collapse. Psychological operations units broadcast instructions on how to surrender properly to coalition forces. The Special Forces teams enjoyed great success, destroying, among other targets, Iraqi border outposts.

Into Iraq

As the decapitation strike against Saddam and his sons ended in uncertainty, the invasion went ahead, in four phases. The first of these was the seizure of the southern Iraqi oil fields, the isolation of the city of Basra, and the securing of bridges across the Euphrates River near the town of Nasiriyah; it was also hoped that this opening move, into the heartland of Iraq's Shi'a majority—a population long oppressed by Saddam—might trigger the collapse of the regime. These initial ground operations were complemented by the large-scale, "shock and awe" air campaign, directed at regime targets in Baghdad and Iraqi military command nodes. Finally, the conventional invasion was supplemented by a huge special operations campaign, a focus of which was denying the Iraqis the use of their western desert to conduct Scud missile launches of the kind that had proved so troublesome in Desert Storm.

On March 20, 2003, the land attack got under way in full force. As in Operation Desert Storm, the army's first large-scale "ground" attack of

Operation Iraqi Freedom was delivered by AH-64 Apache attack helicopters striking Iraqi border outposts. And indeed, these eleven targets—fixed guard positions—had been softened up by artillery strikes just prior to the Apache raid. Once the observation posts had been destroyed, the thousands of vehicles of the Third Infantry Division began streaming through the ten lanes cut in the border sand berm. Major General Buford Blount's first and second brigades quickly established a toehold inside Iraq and prepared to pass through the Third Squadron, Seventh Cavalry—the division's primary force for reconnaissance and security—and the Third Brigade, under Colonel Daniel Allyn. These two units would lead the drive toward Tallil Airfield, just outside the town of Nasiriyah.[3]

Nasiriyah was the first key objective in the ground maneuver scheme. It marked a crucial potential crossing point on the Euphrates, where the main highway running north from Kuwait diverted east and crossed the river in two spots, one several miles northwest and one right in the heart of the city. Seizing at least one Euphrates bridge was important to speed the marines' supporting attack; it was also a spot where U.S. forces would be vulnerable to counterattack and to chemical strikes. The large airfield at Tallil just west of Nasiriyah was key to defending the bridge and the city and, conversely, a good jumping-off point for further U.S. thrusts.

The assault on Tallil reflected the close marriage of joint firepower and maneuver that would come to characterize Operation Iraqi Freedom: Special Forces had been inserted prior to the Third Infantry Division's main attack and had provided precision targeting of Iraqi units and positions defending the airfield; autonomously guided artillery rounds had picked out individual tanks and other vehicles. Apaches and artillery then scouted toward the bridge and suppressed whatever resistance was nearby, and soon the Third Brigade's armor had overrun the airfield. Colonel Allyn then sent forward one of his task forces, Second Battalion, Sixty-ninth Armor, to seize the bridge itself.[4]

The initial marine attack was a three-pronged thrust north from Kuwait. The First Marine Expeditionary Force, or I MEF, was acting essentially as a corps-level command, like the Army's V Corps, although it also directed the firepower of the Third Marine Air Wing, with Cobra attack helicopters, AV-8B Harrier jump-jets, and F/A-18 strike fighters. The I MEF's role vis-à-vis the British First Armoured Division was more coordination than direct command; the British would fight their own tactical battles. The main marine strike force was the First Marine Division, bolstered by virtually the Corps' entire complement of tanks and Light Armored Vehicles.

The division's three Regimental Combat Teams, built around the first, third, and seventh marine infantry regiments, each roughly the strength of an army brigade, provided the three prongs of the initial attacks. The Seventh Regimental Combat Team, "RCT-7" in marine parlance, took the easternmost route, hooking around the Iraqi border town of Safwan and then heading northeast towards Basra. This axis lead RCT-7 through the vital Rumailah oil fields. The hope was to capture the oil fields intact, before Saddam Hussein had a chance to sabotage them. Key within the infrastructure was a pumping station near the town of Az Zubayr, about halfway between Safwan and Basra. The marines dubbed this the "Crown Jewel" of the oil fields.

> In mid-March the Az Zubayr pumping station was generating over $40 million a day. If Saddam blew the turbines [which powered the station], the station would not resume operating for a year. One single pumping station was worth billions— money the U.S. taxpayer would not have to pay to rebuild Iraq if the Crown Jewel was taken intact.[5]

The First Battalion, Seventh RCT, captured Az Zubayr intact and secured it by March 22, brushing aside elements of the Fifty-first Iraqi Armored Division that were positioned less than two miles away. With the British making for Basra, the regiment then turned around and prepared for the march to Baghdad.[6]

On the opposite, western marine flank and linked in with the army was the First RCT. When the ground campaign began, the regiment struck out from Kuwait across the desert northwest toward the town of Jalibah. Also on the western flank was another powerful marine unit, dubbed "Task Force Tarawa." In the center of the First Marine Division was the Fifth RCT. Its initial attack skirted the western edge of the Rumailah oil fields, leading it to the northwest out of Kuwait. Once reaching Highway 8 just southwest of the town of Rumailah, the regiment turned away from the oil fields, following behind the First RCT. The three prongs of the First Marine Division had secured their initial objectives and then turned ninety degrees left, preparing to surge to the river crossing sites in Nasiriyah.

In the south, the British Third Commando Brigade and the U.S. Fifteenth Marine Expeditionary Unit assaulted the al Faw peninsula to secure oil facilities and the port of Umm Qasr. These attacks were quite successful: "Over half the Iraqi oil production, approximately 1.6 million barrels per day produced by the 1,074 Rumailah oil wells, has been secured for the Iraqi people," declared Lieutenant General James Conway, commander of the First Marine Expeditionary Force.

The rest of the British First Armoured Division, with a total strength of about 20,000 soldiers, attacked toward Basra and the Iraqi Fifty-first Mechanized Infantry Division. The British division was really an ad hoc grouping of the Seventh Armoured Brigade, the Sixteenth Air Assault Brigade, and the Third Commando; like U.S. forces, the rushed deployment had forced London to take logistic risks. Moreover, the Turks' refusal to allow Coalition forces to deploy in the north had also complicated British planning. Luckily, a 2001 training mission in Oman, Exercise Saif Sareea II, had helped the British prepare for the war in important ways, including a rapid and expensive program to "desertize" their Challenger II tanks. Nonetheless, while the British were assuming a crucial role in their mission to Basra, and the addition of the Fifteenth Marine Expeditionary Unit would add an extra battalion of infantry and firepower, they were stretched near their limits.

The British plan of attack, generally along the right flank of the I MEF, sent the U.S. Marines and the Third Commando Brigade toward the al Faw peninsula and to the port town of Umm Qasr, along the Shatt al Arab waterway where the Tigris and Euphrates empty into the Persian Gulf. The thrust toward Basra would be spearheaded by the Seventh Armoured Brigade, which passed through the marine lines. The British tanks successfully sprinted the seventy miles to the outskirts of Basra. At that point, the British were essentially on their own.[7]

But like their American allies, and with a relatively small force, the British were reluctant to be drawn into the streets of Basra. As U.S. planners intended to do around Baghdad, the British established a loose cordon around the southern town.

Because it was difficult to assess the Iraqi reaction to the decapitation strike, the air campaign unfolded slowly. Targets for the second night, March 20, included a compound used by senior Iraqi leaders, struck by Tomahawk cruise missiles. Air-defense suppression continued, along with missile systems and artillery that might be able to strike coalition forces in Kuwait. The air assault ramped up even further on the night of March 21, with more than 1,700 air sorties and 500 air- and sea-launched cruise missile strikes.[8]

That day, Defense Secretary Rumsfeld appeared before the press and delivered a statement of eight goals for the war now underway:

> Coalition military operations are focused on achieving several specific objectives: to end the regime of Saddam Hussein by striking with force on a scope and scale that makes clear to Iraqis that he and his regime are finished.
>
> Next, to identify, isolate and eventually eliminate Iraq's weapons of mass destruction, their delivery systems, production capabilities and distribution networks.
>
> Third, to search for, capture, drive out terrorists who have found safe harbor in Iraq.
>
> Fourth, to collect such intelligence as we can find related to terrorist networks in Iraq and beyond.
>
> Fifth, to collect such intelligence as we can find related to the global network of illicit weapons of mass destruction activity.
>
> Sixth, to end sanctions and to immediately deliver humanitarian relief, food and medicine to the displaced and to the many needy Iraqi citizens.
>
> Seventh, to secure Iraq's oil fields and resources, which belong to the Iraqi people, and which they will need to develop their country after decades of neglect by the Iraqi regime.

And last, to help the Iraqi people create the conditions for a rapid transition to a representative self-government that is not a threat to its neighbors and is committed to ensuring the territorial integrity of that country.[9]

Piercing Saddam's Shield

The second phase of the conventional campaign marked a two-pronged march to the outskirts of Baghdad, by the Army's V Corps for the most part west of the Euphrates, and by the First Marine Expeditionary Force east of the river. In addition, a small airborne brigade, along with Special Forces, conducted an economy-of-force mission in northern Iraq, working with the Kurdish resistance and U.S. air forces to strike at important targets. Meanwhile, to the south, the focus of the air campaign swung toward the armored brigades of the Republican Guard, which were arrayed in an arc below Baghdad.

While this second phase of operations was also strikingly successful, it was complicated by a raging sandstorm and by often suicidal resistance from Iraqi irregulars, notably the Saddam fedayeen. In retrospect, these attacks were not militarily significant, but may have had a larger strategic effect. The combination of guerrilla attacks and terrible weather was amplified by television coverage, both in the West and around the Arab world, which suggested that the coalition attack was bogged down. The impression that Iraqi resistance was tougher than expected lingers to this day and continues to cloud assessments of the military situation in Iraq.

On the third and fourth days of the ground campaign, March 22 and March 23, 2003, the army and Marine Corps advanced past the town of Jalibah and toward the major crossing sites near Nasiriyah. The Third Infantry Division had seized the bridges north of the city, on Iraqi Route 1, and prepared to pass the marines through to the east of the river. Although a single crossing site would form a bottleneck that might slow the advance, seizing a second set of bridges to the south would require the marines to make their way through the center of town; the ground campaign plan had hoped to stay out of built-up urban areas wherever possible to reduce the vulnerability of supply columns. Marine planners referred to this road as "Ambush Alley."[10]

Yet Nasiriyah, a city of about 400,000, had been a center of the Shi'ite uprisings of 1991, and intelligence assessments were that the Iraqi Eleventh Infantry Division, garrisoning the town, would either surrender en masse or refuse to fight. Thus marine planners elected to chance a second crossing through Nasiriyah and then drive northward along Iraqi Route 7, yet another of the large highways built by Saddam. The marine plan was to assault through Nasiriyah with Task Force Tarawa, which would hold the bridges and then pass through the First Regimental Combat Team. The Seventh and Third RCTs would use the northern bridges held by the army.

Initially, both crossings went relatively smoothly and indeed, the Iraqi regular forces put up little resistance. However, irregular forces, including substantial numbers of the Saddam fedayeen, had moved into the area and began to organize guerrilla attacks. Soon, Task Force Tarawa found itself in constant combat with the Iraqi irregulars, suffering significant casualties. Following behind Tarawa, the marines in the First RCT were also heavily engaged. "Ambush Alley" was living up to its name.

And even though the V Corps attack was proceeding well, Iraqi irregulars were starting to make themselves felt as the corps advanced. The Third Infantry Division had passed its Third Brigade into the lead, screened by the divisional cavalry squadron, the Third Battalion, Seventh Cavalry Regiment. Past Nasiriyah, the division and the corps troops supporting it embarked upon a three-day march that would take them past the Euphrates towns of Samawah and Najaf, to a space in the desert code-named Objective Rams, which would be the jumping-off spot for the attack against the Republican Guard and into Baghdad. The division plodded along two corridors, appropriately dubbed Hurricane and Tornado.

As the march neared Samawah, the Iraqi attacks increased, and now included relatively accurate artillery and mortar fire in addition to the ambushes and suicide dashes of the fedayeen. None of these attacks proved particularly successful—the division's own howitzers returned highly accurate counterbattery fire against the Iraqi mortars and cannon—but the guerrillas were becoming a potential threat to the lengthening line of supply. The Iraqi tactics were helped by the worsening weather, which was developing into a full-blown sandstorm that limited visibility to a few yards. This allowed attackers with rocket-propelled grenades to sneak in closer to U.S. positions and convoys, or further obscure their hiding spots for ambushes. And soon the division would have to pause to refuel; the decision to delay the deployment of supply units limited the operational range of the armored spearhead. In midafternoon, the First Brigade of the Third Infantry Division established a blocking position along Iraqi Highway 9 north of Najaf.[11] Soon 230 fuelers would begin dispensing gas to M1 tanks with nearly empty gas tanks.

The V Corps attack was running out of steam as well as gas. Soldiers were exhausted after days of bumper-to-bumper convoys, working their way through choking dust for hundreds of miles. Division commander Major General Buford Blount decided that simply bypassing Najaf, a city of half a million and one of two major Shi'a holy cities, would be a mistake. He wanted to surround the town from the north and west to prevent guerrilla infiltrations, and on March 25 sent the 3/7 Cavalry to seize the bridge over the Euphrates north of Najaf to complete the blocking positions.

Moreover, continuing fights with the Saddam fedayeen and other irregular forces in Nasiriyah, Samawah, and Najaf were diverting combat power. The Third Infantry Division was spread out from Samawah, where the tail end of its Third Brigade was providing rear-area security, to the north of Najaf, where the lead elements of the First Brigade were blocking the town from the north and fighting for a bridge over the Euphrates. The Second Brigade was surrounding the city. Unless these units were rearmed, refueled, and reorganized, the main attack toward Baghdad would lack much punch, and the run through the Karbala Gap would be a dangerous, piecemeal effort.

Blount's superior, V Corps commander Lieutenant General William S. Wallace, did not want to make this attack until he was ready and could sustain it. He drew no distinction between the fight for the Karbala Gap and the move to surround Baghdad; once he sent the V Corps—meaning the Third Infantry Division—through the three-kilometer-wide neck of land between the city of Karbala and Lake Razaza, he did not want to stop. To prepare for the attack, however, Wallace wanted to "set the corps" and to build three to six days' of supplies at Objective Rams outside Najaf.[12]

McKiernan concurred, and suggested that the brigade of the Eighty-second Airborne—the element intended to exploit "catastrophic success" by securing Baghdad if Saddam's regime had collapsed at the outset of the war—be diverted to secure Samawah and that the 101st Airborne—the reserve intended to strike deep and surround Baghdad—also help to secure the long line of communication. The opportunity cost of these decisions, however, was that there would not be much left to reinforce the Third Infantry Division if it ran into trouble. And employing the 101st Airborne to help with the cordoning of Baghdad would be problematic; although the division's troop transport helicopters would allow it to move rapidly to cut off escape routes to the north, extricating the division's infantry from its missions to secure the cities in the rear would take time.

There was also the question of how to coordinate the army and marine attacks toward Baghdad. Despite the struggle to get through Nasiriyah, the I MEF and the First Marine Division had made good progress along Iraqi Route 1 once across the Euphrates. If V Corps paused, what should Conway's marines do? Should they continue to move northward, or should they also pause?[13]

Further, the intelligence picture, particularly on Saddam's fedayeen, Special Republican Guard, and other irregular forces, remained unclear. These forces had fought hard in the south and continued menacing attacks in and around Nasiriyah, Samawah, and Najaf. The level of resistance in Karbala and, particularly, in Baghdad, was uncertain, but it seemed probable that the guerrilla and suicide attacks would continue. There was also the question of the heavy forces of the Republican Guard, which were only now coming under significant air attack.

A final consideration was how the media were covering the guerrilla attacks, the sandstorm, and the persistence of Saddam's regime despite the air strikes in Baghdad. In particular, the cable news channels that thrived on crises were beginning to hint that the land campaign was bogged down.

But while V Corps needed a break to recover from its race to Objective Rams and set itself for the attack on Baghdad, other elements of the ground attack were proceeding well. The 173rd Airborne Infantry Brigade had successfully jumped into Kurdistan, consolidating and expanding operations with the *peshmerga* and directing air attacks. British forces patrolled along the al Faw peninsula and had raided Ba'ath party headquarters in Basra, slowly but relentlessly collapsing resistance in the deep south. And while irregular attacks continued on marine convoys in Nasiriyah, most of the I MEF had cleared or bypassed the town; the marines were racing toward their intermediate objectives at Diwaniyah and Kut, and their logistics situation was fairly good. While Conway consented to the pause, he would have been able to continue the marine attacks if required.

Most importantly, CENTCOM had other means to keep the pressure on the Iraqis. While the ground campaign paused, the air campaign began to focus in earnest on the Republican Guard, shifting the balance of its strike sorties against Iraqi forces in the field and on the outer defensive ring around Baghdad. While the sandstorm limited visibility on the ground, the radars and other sensors on air force reconnaissance aircraft could still find targets. Indeed, the difficulty was to distinguish moving vehicles that might hold fleeing civilians from those carrying Saddam fedayeen. The volume of traffic remained terrific even as Saddam's perimeter was collapsing, and the mixing bowl of Baghdad might even have hidden armored formations moving southward to respond to the ground attacks.

The Iraqi Freedom air campaign was different from Desert Storm, as was the ground campaign. For one, no-fly-zone operations had "shaped" the Iraqi air defenses for nearly a decade and, in the weeks just prior to Iraqi Freedom—even as diplomats were making their final attempts to avoid the war—air strikes had begun to hit an expanded set of targets. But whereas the Desert Storm air campaign had spent weeks focused on "strategic" targets in Baghdad and elsewhere, the Iraqi Freedom air war was much more closely integrated with the land attacks. Even the "shock and awe" strikes that opened the campaign did not last that long; by the night of March 22, the coalition air forces had shifted to a more flexible set of missions, with pilots only receiving their targets after takeoff. The number of cruise missile attacks also dropped precipitously.

In retrospect, it appears that even the *shamal* sandstorm that blew up on March 25 was a blessing in disguise. Believing that the reduced visibility would shield their movements, the Iraqis hurried to reposition their land forces to block the V Corps and marine advances in the south. But while attack helicopters and close air support aircraft were limited by the storm, higher flying reconnaissance aircraft, long-range unmanned aerial vehicles, bombers, and strike fighters could employ their radars and thermal systems to locate and attack targets through the storm. As Robert Scales and Williamson Murray have reported:

> Lieutenant Colonel Robert Givens, operations officer of the 524th Fighter Squadron, [a unit] equipped with F-16s, was able to use his on-board infrared sensors to pick up a group of Iraqi vehicles whose movement Army drones had detected. Givens then dropped his 500-pound [bombs] destroying eight tanks and infantry fighting vehicles belonging to the Republican Guard Medina Division. During heavy fighting near Najaf, [unmanned aerial vehicles] and [Joint Surveillance Targeting and Reconnaissance System aircraft] picked up a compact formation of Iraqi T-72 tanks and other armored vehicles moving forward to attack. Four [Global Positioning System]-guided bombs were sufficient to take out no less than thirty of the vehicles and halt the formation before it could deploy an attack. [14]

Iraqi commanders were presented with an insoluble conundrum: If they remained in their dispersed positions, they would either be bypassed or destroyed by the rapidly advancing army and marine forces; if they moved, they would eventually be discovered by U.S. reconnaissance systems and struck from the air. The Iraqis were never able to muster or coordinate a large-scale defense. But for its fedayeen and other irregulars, Saddam Hussein's regime was all but defenseless.

Yet because the air campaign occurred "off camera," the public perception of the war was wildly out of synch with reality. The fierce sandstorm reduced visibility on the ground to just a few yards and allowed small units and single guerrillas to sneak up to close range against U.S. ground units. However, the sandstorm did not prevent V Corps from readying itself for the thrust into Baghdad. Supplies were flowing into the logistics base at Objective Rams outside Najaf. With no prospect of an immediate surrender by Saddam's government, General Franks had released the Eighty-second Airborne to Wallace to protect V Corps from irregular attacks coming out of Samawah and Najaf, and Wallace further decided to sweep the city with the 101st Airborne.

On March 29, the weather cleared and the air campaign accelerated even further. During the sandstorm, the stage had been set for the assault on Baghdad. Soldiers had gotten much-needed rest, and supplies had been laid in at Objective Rams to allow the Third Infantry Division to renew the attack. Yet the overall correlation of forces was uncertain. Although the various Iraqi irregular forces and Saddam loyalists had shown up much earlier and much farther south than anticipated, intelligence assessments still assumed that such elements, most notably the Special Republican Guard, remained in strength in Baghdad. And while it was reasonable to assume that the heavy pounding from the air had weakened the already-dispersed brigades of the Republican Guard armored force, bomb damage assessments lagged behind the stepped-up air war. Moreover, the massive date-palm groves along the Euphrates probably shielded some of these armored forces from detection and attack.

Perhaps most important, Wallace's attack force, relatively small to begin with, had been depleted by the need to protect V Corps' lines of communication. While the Eighty-second Airborne lacked the mobility or firepower to lead the charge into the Baghdad defenses, its infantry strength might come in handy once in the built-up areas of the city and its suburbs. The diversion of the 101st Airborne was more problematic. It essentially limited Wallace and McKiernan's options to seal off Baghdad from the north, to place ground forces astride the most likely escape route, or to serve as an "anvil" to the armored "hammer" of the Third Infantry Division and the marines.

And Wallace still lacked sufficient force to conduct the three-pronged attack from the south that he had hoped for in planning. There were three approaches to Baghdad. From the southeast, the marines would attack in two columns up Route 1 and Route 7, circling the town of Kut and converging at Numaniyah before continuing along the east bank of the Tigris to Baghdad. From the southwest, the Third Infantry Division would sprint through the Karbala Gap, and then cross the Euphrates to the Baghdad airport and into the city; having fought the sand and the fedayeen in the desert, the division now had the shortest final march. But the most direct route to Baghdad, along Route 8, would go uncovered. There were advantages to avoiding Route 8; it ran astride the densest Republican Guard defenses. But conversely, simply bypassing those positions might leave the Guard's mounted forces freedom to maneuver against either the V Corps or marine flanks and rear. While U.S. air power would mitigate the danger, some risks remained.

Wallace's solution was to conduct a feint toward the Route 8 corridor, seeking to draw Iraqi attention to this direct axis of approach toward Baghdad. First of all, the left prong of the marine march, along Route 1 toward Diwaniyah, reinforced the suggestion that the Americans would go straight for the capital. But once at Diwaniyah, and rather than fighting through the complex terrain between Diwaniyah and Hillah, the marines would turn due east to Numaniyah. Second, the cavalry squadron of the Third Infantry Division, the Third Squadron, Seventh Cavalry Regiment, would cross the Euphrates and conduct a show of force intended to further focus Iraqi attention. Finally, even as it secured the city of Najaf, the 101st Airborne would conduct a raid into the town of Hillah, the last major point of Route 8, before it entered the Baghdad region. While these three feints could not have the effect of even a secondary attack in terms of drawing Iraqi forces—and in particular, drawing the Republican Guard away from the Karbala Gap—it was a demonstration Wallace believed vitally important.

In all, the Iraqi Freedom land campaign was choreographed far better than the Desert Storm ground war. Not only were greater ends achieved with far fewer means, but the various elements of the land attack were better synchronized with both the air campaign and one another. While most commentary and Pentagon attention has focused on the jointness of the air-land campaign, the sophistication of the ground war itself is equally striking. During Desert Storm, not only were separate air and land wars fought, but the marines and two army corps also fought essentially three poorly coordinated land attacks.

In 1991, General Schwarzkopf insisted upon acting as his own "land component commander," as well as performing the overall duties of a theater commander-in-chief: placating the massive and disparate Desert Storm coalition, dealing with superiors in Washington, appearing before the media, coordinating the land and air wars, and so on. Part of the result was that the land attacks were poorly conceived. The campaign's two goals—to liberate Kuwait and "destroy" the armored forces of the Republican Guard—were somewhat at odds; at least they demanded very different schemes of maneuver. Schwarzkopf solved this puzzle by attempting to conduct an encirclement of the Republican Guard through the famous "left hook" maneuver—which was itself a two-pronged assault led by the Army's XVIII Airborne and VII Corps—while sending the marines directly to Kuwait City.

While each of these assaults was quite successful in its own right, the whole was less than the sum of the parts. Believing that the marines, although they had the nearest objective, would have the toughest fight, Schwarzkopf attacked first toward Kuwait. The left hook was to follow a day later, but when the marines enjoyed great initial success, Schwarzkopf tried to speed up the army attacks. Although this was a correct decision, the timing of the three attacks had become problematic. The marines were driving the Iraqis into a general retreat—symbolized by the so-called "highway of death" north of Kuwait City—collapsing the Iraqi defenses before the army's armored forces had a chance to complete the encirclement. Moreover, the Army's Twenty-fourth Infantry Division (which, ironically, had been redesignated as the Third Infantry Division during the defense drawdown of the 1990s), which had the longest march and was to "close the noose" on the Republican Guard by sealing off the Euphrates, was the last to cross its line of departure. The poorly synchronized land campaign, along with the inability of air power to seal off the line of the Euphrates completely, limited the value of the Desert Storm victory.

For Operation Iraqi Freedom, theater commander Franks had wisely resisted the lure of acting as his own overall land commander. Instead, he gave that job to McKiernan, who was able to move forward to meet with subordinate tactical commanders, creating his own "feel" for how the fight was progressing and ensuring that his intent was clearly understood.

Still, McKiernan's task was difficult. The lack of a mobile armored force in the north meant that there could be no complete operational encirclement of the Iraqis. True, the ability of air power to limit movement by large-scale forces had improved since 1991 with improved reconnaissance and precision-strike capabilities, and Special Forces roamed Iraq's western desert increasingly at will and were better integrated into the overall campaign. But the fact remained that there would be a relatively open route running north and west from Baghdad through the Sunni heartland and toward the Syrian border.

Further, the attack on Baghdad itself would recapitulate this problem on a smaller scale. The need to commit both the theater reserve force—the brigade of the Eighty-second Airborne that had been intended to exploit an early collapse of the regime—and the V Corps reserve—the 101st Airborne—to securing the cities along the Euphrates and dealing with the problems caused by the Saddam fedayeen and other irregular forces meant that it would be impossible to seal off the city immediately.

McKiernan, Wallace, and First Marine Division commander Major General Mike Mattis solved this puzzle as best they could, synchronizing the marine and army attacks to try to focus Iraqi attention on the marine attacks from the southeast. By suggesting that the army would come up Route 8, the most direct route to Baghdad, while trying to slip the Third Infantry Division in through the Karbala Gap, the "side door" to Baghdad and the Republican Guard line of defenses, it was vital to build the timing of the attack around the latter maneuver, to prevent the problems of success from unhinging the plan—as had happened in Desert Storm. If the marines had continued their attacks through the pause and the sandstorm, while V Corps was rearming and refueling, chances were good that they would already be at the gates of Baghdad, at the Diyalah River. The one chance for a decisive maneuver and at least a partial encirclement was by slicing through the Karbala Gap and continuing the attack without pause into Baghdad—puncturing the Iraqi defenses rather than crumbling them all along the line.

On to Baghdad

Penetrating the Karbala Gap was the key to the third phase of the ground campaign, which would not end until the fall of Saddam Hussein's statues from Firdos Square and elsewhere in Baghdad. Moreover, the Karbala Gap had become, in the years after Desert Storm, one of the most intensely studied pieces of terrain in the world of U.S. military planners—the Iraqi version of the Fulda Gap on the central German plain, the obsessive object of generations of Cold War planners. This terrain, even more than the Iraqi resistance itself, would shape the nature of the main approach to Baghdad. Robert Scales, who recently retired as the commandant of the Army War College and who had overseen the service's official Desert Storm history, captures well in his book with Williamson Murray the nearly mythic stature of the Karbala Gap's ground:

> Virtually every American army officer knew about the gap from war games and exercises as far afield as Fort Hood, Texas and Grafenwoehr, Germany, because the city of Karbala represented the gateway to Baghdad. The area around the Euphrates where the 3rd Infantry Division planned to cross the river was a nightmare of bogs and obstacles, all made more forbidding by the competent work of Iraqi military engineers. Immediately to the north of Karbala lay a huge reservoir. If the Iraqis managed to blow the Haditha Dam, the resulting flood would make an armored advance impossible. Even if they left the reservoir intact, the Iraqis would try to demolish the Karbala bridges.
>
> Thus, several critical tasks confronted [generals] Wallace and Blount if [the] 3rd Infantry Division were to cross the gap successfully. The first had to do with terrain. The Haditha Dam had to be captured. The original plan called for army rangers to secure the dam before moving on. That changed when [theater commander] Franks ordered the dam held until instructed otherwise. This resulted in a two-week battle, in which the rangers fended off determined Iraqi attacks and endured heavy shelling. They were eventually relieved by the 101st Airborne. The second critical task for the 3rd Infantry Division was to seize a river crossing point and move brigade combat teams through the gap so quickly the Iraqis would have no opportunity to use chemical weapons. If Saddam were going to launch [weapons of mass destruction], this was the place to do it: American troops would be concentrated and the gap was far enough distant from Baghdad to avoid collateral damage.[15]

The pause had also permitted Third Infantry Division Commander Blount to reassemble his scattered brigades, with the Eighty-second

Airborne relieving Blount's Third Brigade around Samawah, which then slotted in behind the division's first and second brigades, which would lead the attack into the Karbala Gap. Though the V Corps reserves had been almost entirely committed to securing the Euphrates towns, plenty of firepower was on call to support the Third Infantry's final thrust. When the weather cleared on March 29 and especially on March 30, the air force had again stepped up its aerial pounding of the Republican Guard mounted forces. Although some Iraqi forces moved to reinforce the defensive line south of Baghdad (and indeed, some had started moving weeks ago when it became clear that there would not be a major coalition armored attack in the north of Iraq), Saddam's generals could not mount more than a piecemeal defense.

When the Third Infantry Division launched its attack into the Karbala Gap on April 1, 2003, the fixed-wing air attacks were supplemented with a massive artillery barrage and by the division's Fourth Brigade, with its Apache attack helicopters, flying armed reconnaissance in front of the lead ground elements. It was not until Colonel David Perkins's Second Brigade was within yards of the Euphrates bridge at Hindiyah—well past the Karbala Gap and the town of Karbala—that it finally encountered organized resistance from the Republican Guard. As much as any piece of terrain, the bridge at Hindiyah was the key to the attack on Baghdad; if captured intact, U.S. forces would have kicked down Saddam's door. That the Third Infantry Division got so close to this vital choke point before hitting the main Republican Guard line of defenses is a measure of the effectiveness of U.S. airpower—which made it virtually impossible for Iraqi mounted forces to move or to mass—and the speed of the advance on land.

As in Desert Storm, Republican Guard heavy forces were more than willing to fight; once the Americans were on them, they held their ground tenaciously and not without some tactical skill. And the terrain around the gap was constricted by marshy ground to the north of the city and in the gap itself below Haditha Dam, and by the streets and buildings of the city to the south. Division Commander Blount attacked with his Second Brigade to the north, punching through the gap and heading for the Euphrates, the First Brigade in the south. The Third Brigade followed after the Second Brigade in the north and held the gap open for supply lines by sealing off the city from the main route that ran through the gap.

With few paved roads through the gap, protecting the division's logistics trains would be critical to sustaining the attack on into Baghdad.

The initial assault on the Hindayah bridge fell to a task force built around the Third Battalion, Sixty-ninth Armored Regiment, commanded by Lieutenant Colonel J. R. Sanderson. Iraqi military engineers had wired the bridge with explosives—why the Iraqis did not blow other Euphrates bridges is a mystery—and, as Sanderson's force approached, detonated their charges. But the bridge did not collapse. Now American engineers from the Third Infantry Division raced to sever the lines leading to the remaining charges, destroy the Iraqi positions immediately on the far side of the bridge, and assess whether the structure was still strong enough to bear the division's seventy-ton M1 tanks. Blount covered his bets by racing three companies of 3/69 Armor across the Hindiyah bridge—like many structures in Iraq, adorned with a painting of Saddam—while ordering his engineers to construct a second span with girders and a third with pontoons alongside.[16]

To the great relief of Blount, Wallace, and McKiernan, the assault through the Karbala Gap to seize the Euphrates bridge had gone far better than anticipated. There had been, again, smaller-scale attacks by Republican Guard dismounted infantry, fedayeen, and other irregulars, and some counterattacks by Iraqi mounted elements. But this initial assault had taken just twenty-four hours to pierce the final Republican Guard shield of Baghdad. As Wallace later told James Kitfield of the *National Journal:* "At that point, I was pretty confident we had Saddam by the balls. . . . I knew we were essentially home free."[17]

The success of the Third Infantry Division and V Corps was inseparable from the marine attacks to the east. Once free of "Ambush Alley" in Nasiriyah, the I MEF continued its advance along two main axes. One crossed the Euphrates just north of Nasiriyah along Iraqi Route 1, which veered northwest away from the river, which flowed west through south-central Iraq. Two elements of the First Marine Division attacked in this direction; the Fifth Regimental Combat Team was in the lead, followed by the First RCT. The second avenue of attack was spearheaded by Task Force Tarawa, followed by the third element of the First Marine Division, the Seventh RCT. Task Force Tarawa had the toughest time in clearing Nasiriyah—and nor were the ambushes ended when the trailing regiment passed through the city—but then drove almost due north along Iraqi Route 7.

The attack along Route 1, which, once past Nasiriyah, ran through relatively sparsely populated areas, proceeded rapidly. The marines' next objective was the town of Diwaniyah, about seventy-five miles up Route 1. Not only was Diwaniyah a city of 420,000, but it was where Iraqi Route 17, a major east-west artery, intersected Route 1 and linked it to Najaf in the west and to the Route 17 corridor—the path of the other marine attack. If the Iraqis had any hopes of hitting either of the marine assaults in the flank, or even moving forces west to Najaf, Route 17 would be an important line of communication. In addition, the city of Afak, with 100,000 residents, lay just to the east of Diwaniyah.[18]

Moreover, an even more important road network stood about twenty-five miles north of Diwaniyah. The marines called this "the Elbow," the intersection where Route 1 met Route 8—the most direct route to Baghdad—and Route 27, which ran east, linking to the Tigris River valley. Route 27, which the marines planned to use to unite their force for the assault into Baghdad, essentially ran right along the Republican Guard defenses. As the Karbala Gap was crucial for V Corps, "the Elbow" was a key terrain feature to the I MEF.

The fifth and seventh marine regiments pushed quickly up Route 1, meeting little organized resistance until the outskirts of Diwaniyah. With fewer tanks and support vehicles and better roads to work with, the marines had fewer logistics problems than V Corps but, at the same time, I MEF was already operating hundreds of miles inland. As Bing West and retired Marine Major General Ray Smith observed in *The March Up*:

> To move continuously so far forward had taken months of preparation and a radical paring down of the division's normal supplies. With the full concurrence of [I MEF commander] Lieutenant General Conway before the war, [1st Marine Division commander] Major General Mattis had stripped down the weight and baggage of the division. In 2001, as a brigadier general, Mattis had taken a reinforced battalion 800 kilometers from ships in the Indian Ocean to a dirt airstrip in Afghanistan—no small feat. The logistics officer from that extended operation was now supervising the division's logistics.[19]

Yet the marine move into Iraq was far larger in scope than the Afghanistan operation: fully half its infantry; more than half its artillery; every tank, light armored vehicle, and amphibious assault vehicle; and elements of all three marine forward support groups.[20] To a force organized, trained, and equipped for the constant sea-duty that is the marines' current core mission, Operation Iraqi Freedom was a massive distortion of standard operating procedures. It is a testament to the Corps that it handled its attacks so superbly, but it is also a metric of the relatively small complement of U.S. ground forces—either army or marine—that such extraordinary measures were required, even to execute an invasion where the force had been intentionally restricted in size.

Once the First Marine Division's lead elements neared Diwaniyah and the intersection of Route 1 and Route 17, they had to slow their northward march to secure their flanks to the east and west. To the east was Diwaniyah, headquarters to an Iraqi commando brigade and, as all the larger towns in southern Iraq proved themselves, a nest for fedayeen and other irregular fighters. To the west lay Afak and Budayr, the local Ba'ath party headquarters, both strong points. As the army found at Samawah and Najaf, and as both the army and marines had learned at Nasiriyah, Saddam's regime was still capable of harassing and suicide attacks. The Iraqi guerrillas also knew enough to let the combat spearheads pass and attack the softer-skinned supporting vehicles. Whatever the common Iraqi felt about his liberation by coalition forces, the continued resistance demanded that commanders in all sectors make greater efforts to suppress attacks from urban areas. There would be no rapid bypassing of cities.

The sandstorm and the decision to halt V Corps made these clearing attacks even more vital. Indeed, marine advance elements had passed through the Diwaniyah area and pushed on to "the Elbow," but had to retreat to the Diwaniyah area in order to keep the larger ground campaign synchronized. But there were risks to the marines in stopping; clearing the roads and towns around Diwaniyah would allow the marines to keep the something of the tactical initiative.

At the end of March, as the sandstorm eased and the ground attacks resumed across the front, the marines of the fifth and seventh RCTs again seized "the Elbow" and turned east along Route 27, pushing toward the town of Numaniyah and the bridges across the Tigris. Once across the river and astride Iraqi Route 6, the entire MEF would mass for the final attack into the Baghdad area.

The fight for Numaniyah was in many ways a reprise of the army's attack on Hindiyah; both river crossings were seized almost simultaneously. A town of 75,000, Numaniyah was similar to other settlements along the Tigris and Euphrates floodplains. Though Saddam's engineers had improved on the thousands of years of building that preceded them, the elevated highways above the marshy paddies severely constricted military movements, binding them to the roads. With the Marine Second Tank Battalion in the lead, the Seventh RCT had snaked its way along Route 27, but had not stopped; when again the Iraqis failed to destroy their bridges, the marines' M1s quickly dashed across at Numaniyah, establishing a perimeter on the east side of the river. And, also like the army, the marines quickly built a pontoon bridge to open a second crossing site.[21] The marines were almost ready to begin their final attack on Baghdad.

But before that could happen, Conway and Mattis had to unite their entire force and reduce the Baghdad and Al Nida divisions of the Republican Guard, in and around the stronghold town of Kut. This was where Iraqi Route 7 crossed the Tigris, at a bend in the river. In their fight along Route 7, Task Force Tarawa and the First Regimental Combat Team faced better organized resistance. The highway led the marines toward the left flank of the Republican Guard defensive line, through the city of Qalat Sikar—about halfway between Nasiriyah and Kut. The marines in this eastern axis had fought a number of larger engagements between Nasiriyah and Qalat Sikar, then had held up east of the town during the pause in the ground campaign.

While the Fifth RCT crossed the Tigris at Numaniyah and then feinted from the north, the marines of Task Force Tarawa and the First RCT would assault Kut. For several days, marine strike aircraft had patrolled the area, reducing Iraqi defenses. The Republican Guard divisions in the area had relatively few tanks or heavy weapons and were no better organized or successful than the Guard elsewhere. Resistance was occasionally sharp, but the Iraqis could not organize a large-scale defense. By the night of April 3, the marines would posture themselves to begin the run into Baghdad. While V Corps was kicking in the side door, the marines were knocking at the front door.

Even as the marines and the Army's Third Infantry Division were positioning themselves to enter Baghdad, the situation along the vital supply routes from Kuwait was improving dramatically. The commitment of the 101st Airborne to sweep through Najaf was even more important, both from an operational and strategic standpoint. Not only was the logistics base outside Najaf essential for support of the Karbala Gap attack, but Najaf, a city of 560,000, is, along with Karbala, one of Islam's holiest cities and the site of the shrine of Imam Ali Abi Talib, the son-in-law of the Prophet Mohammed and the fourth caliph. In addition, Najaf houses the preeminent seminary for the training of Shi'ite clerics. Eliminating the grip of Saddam's regime in Najaf, therefore, would be a key to convincing the majority of Iraqis that the United States was serious in its project of transforming the political order of the region.

The 101st Airborne had barely made it to the war on time.[22] The division's commander, Major General Petraeus, had hustled the 18,000 "Screaming Eagles" out of Fort Campbell, Kentucky, in ten days, and less than a month after official deployment notification, the division was beginning to unload its equipment—including more than 250 transport and assault helicopters—from ships docked in Kuwait. As in Desert Storm, when the division conducted a heliborne attack directly from the Saudi border to the middle of the Iraqi desert and then to the Euphrates valley, the 101st was again poised to execute deep strikes, particularly to cordon off Baghdad. But at the start of combat, "G-Day," the division began a long and tedious march in ten convoys totaling more than 2,700 vehicles. Its first objective was to establish a rearming and refueling point, dubbed "Exxon," opposite Nasiriyah, to provide support for the helicopter armada and for other V Corps units. In essence, Exxon was the American military's first gas station inside Iraq—a rest stop on the supply route that ultimately linked Kuwait and Baghdad and pumped more than half a million gallons of fuel in the course of the war.

As with the rest of the initial attacks, the movement to Exxon was successful. The next jump, to create a more robust "forward arming and refueling point" (FARP), was a greater challenge. This FARP Shell was part of the massive complex at Objective Rams outside Najaf, and the division's movement there was complicated by the late March sandstorm and the confusion created by the attacks of Saddam's guerrilla loyalists. Beginning with the initial assault and establishment of a security perimeter on March 22, the 101st consolidated and operated from there over the next two weeks.

Once the decision was made March 26 to pause in the attack toward Baghdad and to secure the rear areas, the 101st focused on the Najaf mission. Despite the continued poor weather, on March 27 the division seized the Euphrates bridge at the village of Kifl, to the north of Najaf, while interdicting the main highway that linked Najaf to Baghdad. Once again, the Iraqis failed to destroy what would prove to be an important river crossing site.

Yet the 101st toehold across the Kifl bridge was tenuous—a single infantry company made the initial assault—and the sandstorm prevented Petraeus from immediately reinforcing the position. And although the Iraqis could not mount a significant ground assault, the Republican Guard units in the area were able to mass their fires. Despite limited visibility, the division's attack helicopter battalion provided constant fire and close air support to the infantry perimeter on the east bank of the Euphrates.[23]

It was not until March 31 that the 101st Airborne was able to renew its move into Najaf. Reinforced by the tanks and Bradley Fighting Vehicles of the Second Battalion, Seventieth Armor, part of the Third Infantry Division, Petraeus planned a two-pronged pincer attack to encircle and isolate the city. The division's Second Brigade crossed at Kifl and swung south along the east bank of the Euphrates, while the First Brigade crossed the river south of Najaf and swung north. With blocking positions still to the west of the city and with armed reconnaissance and attack helicopters—and fixed-wing aircraft as well—providing close fire support, Najaf was sealed tight; the V Corps attack could proceed without worry about its lines of communication, and the people of Najaf could see that the Iraqi regime's grip and the terror of its death squads were coming to an end. The 101st continued to sweep through the streets of Najaf in force until April 3, locating and occupying or destroying Ba'ath Party headquarters and other regime outposts, often going door to door and working with local Iraqis to identify the enemy. And just as often, postcombat stability operations would follow immediately when a neighborhood or district was secured.

In the far south, in the British sector around Basra, the coalition was also enjoying increased success. By the end of March, most of the organized Iraqi army defenses in and around the city had collapsed, and the British had begun to infiltrate the city proper with small teams of special operations forces, snipers, and infantry. However, the British still had some tough tasks ahead and reasons for continued caution: Saddam loyalists and fedayeen were hiding among the local populace, and had no compunction about using the people, mostly Shi'a, as "human shields" or simply to create spectacular atrocities. As the sniper teams took their toll among the Ba'athists, the British undertook larger raids into Basra, using armored vehicles as well as dismounted infantry. British special operations forces also called for precision air attacks, targeting GPS-guided bombs at important targets. But much of the challenge was not strictly military: It was to convince a brutalized Shi'a community that, as a British propaganda leaflet put it, "We will not desert you this time. Trust us and be patient."[24]

As the main ground attacks closed on Baghdad and Basra, and the air campaign continued to destroy what little organized defense the Republican Guard could mount, the one weakness in the overall campaign continued to be the lack of a large mobile force that could close the ring around Baghdad from the north. An American task force, under the command of the Tenth Special Forces Group and including parts of the Third Special Forces Group, had been slowly assembling in Iraqi Kurdistan since mid-February. It had been working with the Kurdish *peshmerga* guerrillas to pin down Iraqi forces along the so-called "Green Line" that defined the limits of Saddam's control in northern Iraq, and to call in air strikes from long-range air force bombers and strike fighters from the carriers *Truman* and *Roosevelt*, stationed in the eastern Mediterranean. The American presence was boosted significantly on March 26 when more than 1,000 paratroopers of the 173rd Airborne Brigade, stationed at Vicenza, Italy, jumped into Bashur airfield in northern Iraq. Working with the Green Berets and *peshmerga* and about twenty air force engineers, the bolstered force rapidly established an expanded perimeter around the base and repaired the runways to receive heavy C-17 transports. Over a period of four days, the U.S. Air Force landed an additional 2,000 troops and—perhaps even more important—nearly 400 vehicles, including a small complement of M1s, Bradleys, and lighter M113 armored personnel carriers.[25]

Though at last the northern invasion force was increasing in strength and tactical mobility, it could never substitute for the sheer power and range of the Fourth Infantry Division—now just beginning to arrive in Kuwait. Moreover, part of the special operations task force mission was to strike at the Ansar al-Islam terrorist camps along the Iranian border. And, of course, the need to soothe Turkish sensibilities about Kurdish independence remained a diplomatic necessity, despite Ankara's refusal to allow the larger force to deploy through its territory. While it is impossible to know with certainty how a northern attack by the Fourth Infantry Division would have materialized, it likely would have had two effects: one, the further demoralization of the Iraqi leadership; and two, a significant effect on the battlefield—not least in the looming assault on Baghdad itself.

Removing the Regime

The final collapse of Saddam Hussein's regime began on April 3, 2003, when Major General Buford Blount's Third Infantry Division began a two-pronged attack on the Baghdad International Airport southwest of the metropolis. The attack through the Karbala Gap had gone far better than Blount expected—so well, in fact, that he thought the Iraqis might have planned to trap his forces in a pocket, and thus he ordered that no wheeled vehicles would cross the Euphrates.[26] The battle for the airport consumed twenty-four chaotic and bloody hours, during which the Iraqis, seemingly awoken at last to the impending end of Saddam's rule, tried vainly to stem the American assault.

The Republican Guard had been swept aside completely. As Lieutenant General Michael Moseley, the senior CENTCOM air commander, said, "Republican Guard units outside Baghdad are now dead. . . . We're not softening them up, we're killing them." The soldiers themselves "are not 100 percent killed," he allowed. "There are still some of them out there. We haven't killed them all but the ones that are still round are walking with a bit of a limp."[27]

The weakness of the Iraqi defenses allowed Blount to reinforce his toehold on the airport throughout the evening, but the Iraqi attacks continued. According to Sean Naylor, a reporter with the *Army Times* embedded with the Third Squadron, Seventh Cavalry Regiment, the divisional cavalry squadron's A Troop "fought a running battle with light infantry militia and suicide bombers through the night and into the morning." Many of the attacks came from cars and buses that charged the U.S.

positions. "Most of the vehicles were found to be manned by uniformed soldiers carrying large sums of cash."[28]

On April 4, the Third Infantry Division moved to complete its control of the airport and to secure the key objective southwest of Baghdad, the intersection of Iraqi Route 1 and Route 8, about seven miles from the city's center. At the airport, the division encountered what appeared to be reinforcements from the Hammurabi Division of the Republican Guard to the west. After calling in air and artillery strikes, the division closed for what became a fierce tank-on-tank encounter with isolated pockets of defenders. Some of these pockets included dozens of armored vehicles. According to Naylor:

> The [divisional cavalry squadron] opened fire with their Abrams [tanks] at ranges of 800 to 1,200 meters. From less than a kilometer away, the fight appeared to be almost completely one-sided. The yellow flashes from [U.S.] tanks were quickly followed by orange fireballs as the high explosive rounds hit home. "There's a lot of shit over there," [a commander] reported over the radio. "We've taken a little bit of fire but most of them are just dying."[29]

By sundown, the Third Infantry Division had secured the airport and was pointed toward the center of Baghdad. The now-familiar mix of Iraqi regular and mounted forces, irregulars, and regime suicide squads continued periodically, but in a piecemeal fashion, to counterattack the airport. But the "loose cordon" of Baghdad was in place in at least one sector southwest of the capital. After two weeks of "shock and awe" air attacks, the Iraqi regime was about to hear the "thunder runs" of heavy ground combat vehicles.

The concept of the "thunder run" had been developed as a potential solution of how to begin to end a siege of Baghdad. Since Desert Storm generals Arnold and Yeosock had first addressed the issue of how to capture the Iraqi capital and remove Saddam Hussein from power more than a decade previously, just how to control a city of 5 million with a small force had remained a puzzle. A bloody, street-by-street battle—or even what looked like one on television—could still undermine the coalition and complicate any attempt to reconstruct postwar Iraq.

Thus a "thunder run" was conceived as a massive raid by tanks and infantry fighting vehicles that would rumble through the streets of central Baghdad, crushing any resistance; American combat vehicles were nearly impervious to the Iraqis' rifles and rocket-propelled grenades. Beyond any direct military impact, the thunder runs would have, it was hoped, a psychological effect, convincing Iraqis that Saddam's end was near and that further fighting would be futile. To underscore the point, the initial thunder run would drive directly into the inner precincts of Baghdad, along the west bank of the Tigris, passing governmental ministries and the public parks that venerated Saddam's rule. The symbols of the regime would be the first targets.

The first thunder run would be the mission of Colonel David Perkins of the Second Brigade of the Third Infantry Division. Perkins in turn summoned Lieutenant Colonel Rick Schwartz, commander of a task force of the First Battalion, Sixty-fourth Armored Regiment.

"At first light tomorrow," Perkins told Schwartz, "I want you to attack into Baghdad."

Schwartz felt disoriented. He had just spent several hours in a tank, leading his armored battalion on an operation that had destroyed dozens of Iraqi tanks and armored vehicles twenty miles south. A hot shard of exploding tank had burned a hole in his shoulder.

"Are you kidding, sir?" Schwartz asked, as he waited for the other officers inside the tent to laugh. There was silence.

"No," said Perkins. "I need you to do this."[30]

Schwartz's "Rogues" began their attack at first light on April 5, surprising Iraqi defenders still eating their breakfast next to stacked arms. After about ten minutes, the fedayeen and other irregulars had begun to pepper the column with small arms fire and occasional rocket-propelled grenade (RPG) shots. Eventually,

> Iraqis turned out in hundreds, literally lining the route, seemingly waiting their turn to die. The Americans obliged. Fighting became particularly surreal as the column approached the center of Baghdad: women and children stood along the street or on rooftops, taking in the carnage before them with the seemingly casual interest of fans watching a soccer match on television.

Equally surreal, [V Corps commander] Wallace watched Perkins' attack first-hand on a Hunter [drone aircraft] downlink
piped into his command center.[31]

The Task Force 1/64 Armor spearhead, about thirty M1 tanks and
fifteen Bradley Fighting Vehicles, was supported by Air Force A-10
"Warthog" close air support aircraft circling in "stacks" above the city, and
by army attack helicopters, "hunting and pecking" for Iraqi positions and
vehicles on Baghdad's side streets. Early in the afternoon, the task force
had completed its circuit of southwestern Baghdad, leaving behind perhaps 2,000 Iraqi dead. Enemy fire had hit nearly every vehicle in the con-
voy and many had been hit repeatedly by RPGs. Yet just one M1 had been
disabled and was later destroyed by an A-10 to prevent its falling into
Iraqi hands; the crew escaped unharmed. The Third Infantry Division's
formal "After Action Report" claimed:

> This war was won in large measure because the enemy could
> not achieve effects against our armored fighting vehicles. . . .
> U.S. armored combat systems enabled the division to close
> with and destroy heavily armored and fanatically determined
> enemy forces with impunity, often within urban terrain.
> Further, the bold use of armor and mechanized forces striking
> at the heart of the regime's defenses enabled the division to
> maintain the initiative and capitalize on the rapid success
> en route to Baghdad. During [military operations in urban
> terrain], no other ground combat system in our arsenal could
> have delivered similar mission success without accepting enor-
> mous casualties.[32]

Ominously, some of the heaviest engagements had occurred well after
Task Force 1/64 had ripped through the center of Baghdad, along the
avenues leading north out of the city—in essence, the escape routes. In
response, division commander Blount dispatched his Third Brigade to
attempt to cover the exits, but the "result was a 10-hour gun battle during
which American soldiers fought off individuals and small teams as well as
large convoys seeking to escape."[33] These engagements included a number

of scrapes with Iraqi tanks and other armored vehicles, and a fight between the divisional cavalry squadron and a Republican Guard unit for the north-ernmost bridge out of central Baghdad left eight Iraqi tanks destroyed. Regime diehards could still slip through the lines, but there was no serious military option left to the Iraqi army in Baghdad west of the Tigris.

Nevertheless, the regime continued to insist in public that its rule con-tinued. Iraqi Information Minister Mohammed Saeed al-Sahef claimed that U.S. forces had not taken the Baghdad airport: "They are not in Baghdad. They are not in control of any airport. . . . It is all a lie. They lie. It is a Hollywood movie."[34] Later, after the information minister reported that Iraqi forces had retaken the Baghdad airport, Republican Guard General Mohammed Daash was sent to investigate whether any American tanks had survived the "counterattack." Daash returned in a panic: "Are you out of your minds? The whole damn American Army is at the airport!"[35]

The Iraqi regime was crumbling. In a teleconference April 6, generals Blount, Wallace, McKiernan, and Franks agreed that the time had come for a larger, more decisive thunder run—indeed, not a raid but a bold move to begin the actual seizure of Baghdad. Again, Perkins's Second Brigade would lead the charge, but this time with double the number of tanks and Bradleys; Task Force 1/64 would be joined by its sister battal-ion, Fourth Battalion, Sixty-fourth Armored Regiment. This would not be a "drive-by shooting," but an attack to seize the regime district up to the Tigris—to occupy Saddam's presidential palace and its grounds—and hold it.

On April 6, the remnants of the Iraqi defenders had tried to block the American way from the airport into central Baghdad, improvising road-blocks from trucks, buses, and a variety of civilian vehicles, and setting ambush sites to hit the U.S. columns as they slowed to clear the roads. Yet it took the lead tanks of Task Force 1/64 Armor just an hour to get into the regime district and for Lieutenant Colonel Schwartz to link up with a special operations team that had infiltrated the city two weeks before.[36] Despite reports of fedayeen massing for suicide attacks, the grand, open boulevards of the district—where Saddam had loved to display his mili-tary might on parade—gave the brigade sufficient fields of fire and good positions to defend. Perkins wanted to stay; Blount agreed without hesi-tation, provided a resupply mission could be completed before dark.

Indeed, over the next twenty-four hours, the crucial factor in occupying Baghdad was not fending off counterattacks in the regime district itself. It was—as so often in the ground campaign—securing the supply lines. The lifeline from the airport to downtown Baghdad led along Iraqi Route 8, which, although a large highway, offered many places for ambushes and hit-and-run attacks. Even more important, three cloverleaf-style ramp intersections had to be held; these were dubbed "Larry," "Moe," and "Curly," after the Three Stooges. It fell to Perkins's Third Battalion, Fifteenth Infantry Regiment, to hold open the line of communication at "Larry" and "Moe" with two infantry company teams of tanks and Bradleys, while "Curly," two miles distant and more isolated, fell to an ad hoc assembly of engineers, infantry, and a mortar platoon, commanded by a battalion staff officer. During the afternoon and evening of April 7, fighting was intense at all three strong points, but most desperate at the "Curly" cloverleaf. Here Syrian irregular fighters and suicide bombers made one of their initial appearances in Iraq, and threatened to overrun the American perimeter. Only by shuttling his B Company, first to "Curly" and then to "Moe," did 3/15 Infantry commander Lieutenant Colonel Steven Twitty manage to hold his objectives. Late in the day, Blount reinforced "Curly" with a full infantry battalion task force from the Third Brigade:

> The successful occupation of Baghdad over the night of April 7–8 essentially broke the back of the Iraqi resistance. A few luckless fedayeen, unaware of the capability of American thermal sights, came out after dark to attack the task forces, only to be shot down immediately by vehicles and soldiers they never saw. By morning, sporadic suicide attacks were all that remained of Iraqi resistance. Even civilians who had been hiding began to emerge to reclaim the dead.[37]

As V Corps pitched its tents in Baghdad, the I Marine Expeditionary Force was about to do the same. After racing up the Mesopotamian valley and crossing the Tigris north of Kut, the lead elements of the First Marine Division turned toward the Iraqi capital, attacking astride Route 6, the "River Road." On April 3, the Marine Fifth Regimental Combat Team was driving the Al Nida Division of the Republican Guard out of its way at the town of Aziziyah, just 60 miles from Baghdad. The regiment's third battalion of infantry was securing the town itself, while the tanks of the Second Tank Battalion rearmed and refueled just outside, to the north.

Route 6 was like other Iraqi highways, roads built with a military purpose in mind, elevated from the surrounding marshy ground and dotted along the way with clusters of buildings, huts, and sand berms. These made excellent ambush sites, but offered no cover for the Iraqis to organize any larger defense—and, as always, any concentration of Iraqi military vehicles drew quick attention from coalition air power. And as the marine ground forces moved toward Baghdad, where the Iraqis were being forced to stand, the carcasses of destroyed Iraqi tanks and Soviet-made BMP infantry fighting vehicles became more common.[38]

The final barrier between the marines and Baghdad was the Diyalah River, which flowed into the Tigris at the southeast corner of the city. Conducting a river crossing in built-up urban terrain doubled the challenge; buildings on the far side of the Diyalah from the marines would provide excellent cover for Iraqi defenders. In addition, the crossing would force marine units to concentrate, increasing their exposure to artillery and mortar fire. Both banks of the river were steep and the Diyalah had few bridges. In the central part of the marines' sector, the river doubled back upon itself.

Major General Mattis, commander of the First Marine Division, decided upon a three-pronged attack. The assault by the Seventh Regimental Combat Team would be aimed at the four-lane Baghdad Bridge just above the junction with the Tigris. The First RCT would be on their right flank, crossing just above the bend in the Diyalah—opposite the Rashid military airport and barracks complex. The Fifth RCT, crossing the Diyalah on a pontoon bridge and keeping with the intent of the ground campaign plan to establish a loose cordon around the city, would circle the outskirts of Baghdad to the north, interdict Iraqi Route 2 and Route 5, then drive southwest through the slums of "Saddam City," the poorest Shi'a part of Baghdad.[39]

The marines attacked into Baghdad on April 7 and by the next day were in control of the streets of the southeast quadrant of the city, conducting clearing operations. Because Baghdad had fallen so rapidly, much of the elaborate planning for urban combat fell with it, and V Corps and I MEF established the Tigris as the boundary between the coalition forces. Soon marines and soldiers were walking the corridors of the palaces of Saddam Hussein, Tariq Aziz, and other senior regime leaders. On April 8, American aircraft began to land at what was no longer Saddam International Airport, but Baghdad International Airport.

Saddam was now a fugitive, and his regime passing into history. On April 9, the famous statue of Saddam in Firdos Square was pulled from its pedestal by Iraqis—with an assist from the marines. Two days later, organized resistance in Baghdad was at an end, at least for the moment. It seemed there was little left but "mopping up" operations, and, as the Bush administration intended, a swift reconstruction of Iraqi government. Defense Secretary Rumsfeld and leaders in the Pentagon also wanted to withdraw U.S. forces as fast as possible and get back to the business of defense "transformation." Rumsfeld was less interested in rearming and refitting the force that had conquered Baghdad in less than three weeks than in restructuring it to face what he believed were changing missions for the future.

PART IV

The Counterinsurgency Campaign

The fourth phase of Operation Iraqi Freedom, the campaign to pacify Iraq and begin its political transformation, has come to dwarf all the operations that preceded it. The price in blood and treasure has been far higher than the invasion itself. More American and allied troops have been killed—indeed, with repeated rotations of fresh formations into the region, more troops have been involved—than in the intense three-week period of major combat operations. The U.S. investment in economic reconstruction is measured in tens of billions of dollars. There is, and will continue to be, a violent rejectionist movement among former regime loyalists, drawn from both the Ba'ath Party and disenfranchised Sunnis, supplemented by criminal gangs and international terrorists of the al Qaeda variety. Not surprisingly, these insurgents are desperate to prevent the development of a free and democratic society in Iraq. There is no immediate prospect of a decisive military victory against this enemy, and the "transfer of sovereignty" after June 30, 2004, is unlikely to reverse the deepening American military involvement in Iraq and the region.

At the same time, there are signs that the pendulum inside Iraq is swinging, albeit slowly and painfully, toward a more hopeful future. The superstructure of Saddam's regime has been destroyed: The dictator is behind bars, his sons are dead, and all but one of his top lieutenants has been captured or killed. The "coalition" of anti-American forces in Iraq is even looser than the U.S.-led alliance and has yet to produce a nation-wide military, let alone political, movement, nor attract a significant state sponsor. Most importantly, the Shi'a majority remains tolerant of the U.S. presence and patiently committed to democracy, as evidenced by Grand Ayatollah Ali al Sistani's endorsement of the new, sovereign government under Prime Minister Iyad Alawi.

In the roughest terms, the postwar insurgency can be divided into three components. The first of these encapsulated the brief moment immediately after the collapse of Saddam's government in April 2003. This proved to be the most fateful "pause" in the invasion, a function of exhausted U.S. forces, policy myopia about the nature of "regime change," and the failure of Turkey to allow the Fourth Infantry Division to open a northern axis of attack into Iraq. While it appeared at the time that the most significant consequence of this pause was the chaos and looting of Iraq, in hindsight it seems clear that it also facilitated the retrenchment of a guerrilla resistance. This would have been perhaps impossible to prevent entirely, but clearly some opportunities to press the advantages won in the major combat campaign were dissipated.

The second component of the insurgency was marked by attempts to attack American and other coalition military forces, striking at the instruments of the occupation but more importantly striking at U.S. public opinion by creating casualties. However, the capture of Saddam was a body blow to the insurgents' strategy—a fact perhaps reflected in the collapse of the campaign of former Vermont Governor Howard Dean for the Democratic Party's presidential nomination.

Faced with this failure to dissuade the United States from its mission in Iraq, the insurgents have also attacked "soft targets" presented by the rest of the international community and those Iraqis working to build a new country. Insurgents staged devastating attacks on the strongest symbols of "neutrality" in Iraq, the United Nations and the International Committee of the Red Cross. Attacks by North African terrorists in Spain helped to defeat the conservative candidate anointed by former President Jose Maria Aznar, who along with Tony Blair was one of the staunchest allies of the Bush administration. The new socialist government in Spain was elected in part on its promise to withdraw Spanish troops from Iraq. In sum, the rejectionists in Iraq have had success in keeping the United States, Britain, and the core coalition members partly isolated from the rest of the international community. While it is hard to judge the long-term strategic significance of this trend, it is perhaps most likely to underscore the disparity of power between the United States and its continental European allies, accelerate American "unilateralism," and frustrate attempts to reform the United Nations to play a more useful role in the post-9/11 world.

But perhaps the most striking failure of the insurgency has been its inability to create the civil war in Iraq that purveyors of conventional strategic wisdom have so feared for more than a decade. Neither the al Qaeda–style Sunni militants nor, for that matter, the Iranians, have been able to provoke Iraq's Shi'a majority—or the Kurds, either—to large-scale violence against each other.

Postwar Chaos

As American forces reached Baghdad, Saddam's totalitarian regime collapsed, and with it, any semblance of law and order. In its place a power vacuum opened—one that U.S. soldiers were neither prepared, directed, nor numerically capable to fill.

Looters stripped government offices, palaces, ministries, and the residences of Ba'athist officials, making off with everything they could carry. Soccer balls were pilfered from youth centers and gasoline sucked from Ba'athist Party automobiles. Initially, much of the pillaging appeared at least partly motivated by a sense of revenge against Saddam's regime, with slogans of Shi'a power painted on walls and government ministries set on fire. But the line between a popular revolt against symbols of the state and mere criminal opportunism quickly blurred, as hospitals, schools, cultural sites, private residences, and foreign embassies were likewise stripped.

The Pentagon initially attempted to brush off the looting as a natural and temporary side-effect of political liberation. "It's untidy," sniffed Secretary Rumsfeld on April 11. "And freedom is untidy. And free people are free to make mistakes and commit crimes." Consequently, the Pentagon insisted that the bulk of U.S. troops would remain fixed on traditional military tasks, such as hunting down regime loyalists, and not such "soft tasks" as policing—which was, in any case, the responsibility of the Office of Reconstruction and Humanitarian Assistance (ORHA) and its chief, Jay Garner, a retired army officer who had led the humanitarian mission to the Kurds after Operation Desert Storm. But if ORHA had the mandate, it lacked the means, having no manpower of its own to quell the looting. Garner and much of his staff, in any case, remained in Kuwait, because (in an impressive display of circular logic) Baghdad was too dangerous.

Meanwhile, U.S. troops adapted to varying degrees, based largely on the initiative and ingenuity of officers on the ground. Ultimately, however, U.S. commanders were not given any clear directive to stop the looting, with General Franks explicitly ruling that soldiers were prohibited from using deadly force to combat it. "The problem is, the people doing the looting are not threatening our forces," explained one Defense Department official. American troops, nonetheless, were dispatched to guard certain elements of the Iraqi infrastructure, such as the oil ministry, as well as to fulfill such "critical" missions as breaking up the mosaic of the first President Bush on the floor of the al Rashid Hotel.

Ultimately, however, even as senior military officials recognized that the looting was indeed a duty that could not be ignored, the division of labor between ORHA and CENTCOM—not to mention the sheer lack of sufficient military manpower on the ground—continued to stymie any attempt at restoring law and order. But soon it became apparent that the security problems posed by postwar Iraq were far larger. What had first appeared to be mere banditry was coalescing into a guerrilla resistance.

The Counterinsurgency

With U.S. occupation forces increasingly the target of attacks, coalition commanders in early June 2003 began a series of large-scale sweeps intended to track down Saddam loyalists and break up insurgent support infrastructure. From the start, these operations were concentrated in what would become known as the "Sunni Triangle," the region north of Baghdad to Tikrit and west to Fallujah and Ramadi. This was not only the hotbed of resistance but also a region largely untouched by the war. Neither the lightly armed airborne force in Kurdistan nor the armored forces that had attacked from Kuwait extended their initial operations quickly or deeply into the region that was Saddam's home.

The first of these sweeps, dubbed Operation Peninsula Strike, began on June 10 and sought to round up Saddamist militia and high-ranking Ba'ath party officials in the town of Thuluya, nestled in groves of date palms along the Tigris River about forty-five miles north of Baghdad. The town was untouched by the war, and U.S. troops rarely entered after combat ended.

This neglect enabled Ba'athists and Saddam fedayeen to take refuge there, coalition leaders believed. Local Iraqis agreed: "Thuluya is the most dangerous place in Iraq," warned Nabel Darwish Mohamed, mayor of the nearby town of Balad. "There are lots of high-ranking Ba'athists, and they have lost their privileges. They will fight back. Also, lots of people have nationalist feelings that the Ba'athists will encourage. It will be easy to find someone to attack Americans."[1]

The sweep was led by the Fourth Infantry Division in conjunction with attached units of the 173rd Airborne Brigade and the Third Infantry Division's cavalry squadron, 3/7 Cavalry, under Task Force Ironhorse. The U.S. Air Force provided cover. A total of approximately four hundred Iraqis were detained, and numerous weapons systems and ammunition were captured.[2]

The commander of a U.S. military police battalion had explained the purpose of the operation quite clearly to the residents of Thuluya: "We met with you last week," said Lieutenant Colonel David Poirier. "We came in peace and only asked that no one try to hurt U.S. forces. That night and the next, people attacked us. Now, we've come in and done what we had to do and the attacks stopped. That's the way it's got to be." It was also clear that American commanders intended these sweeps to be decisive. "There are going to be more of these operations," declared one planner. "They will be intensely coordinated. There will be no sanctuary for the [Saddam] fedayeen or Ba'athists."[3]

Coalition forces also combined increased civic action patrols with the raids, employing classic counterinsurgency tactics even as the country-wide effort to restore public services remained a stop-and-start affair. "We worked hard for every combat action to have a 'carrot' that followed," said Army Colonel David MacEwen. "We'd do a cordon-and-search [operation] in one area, and then make sure the next day that [cooking gas] was available, or that a pump at a water plant was working."[4] Such civil affairs operations also had immense intelligence value. The pattern of operations also helped to reassure—or to intimidate—Iraqis that U.S. forces were going to remain in Iraq until stability and security were established.

Even as Operation Peninsula Strike was being executed, so was an important raid on a camp in northern Iraq where foreign terrorists were gathering, training, and storing supplies. This was conducted by Special

Forces of Task Force 20 and the 101st Airborne against a collection of compounds designated "Objective Snake," about forty miles from the Syrian border. About fifty terrorists were killed in the raid, and several vehicles and numerous munitions, including surface-to-air missiles and huge caches of rocket-propelled grenades, were destroyed. Intelligence gathered in the raid indicated that these fighters intended to move southward toward Ramadi and Fallujah.[5]

American commanders maintained a high pace of operations, launching another large sweep, Operation Desert Scorpion, aimed at cutting off escape routes for fugitive Iraqi leaders. The sweep began with fifty-six simultaneous, large-scale raids in central Iraq and brought in "a hoard of intelligence."[6] Among those captured was Abid Hamid Mahmud, one of Saddam's aides. "He has revealed a lot," a senior army officer told the *Washington Post*. "He knew where all the safe houses and rat lines"—escape routes—"were."[7]

The pressure continued with Operation Sidewinder, a series of more than twenty simultaneous raids on suspected weapons and ammunition caches, as well as resistance leaders, in the belt along the Tigris River through the Sunni region, from the town of Samarra to Baghdad.[8] The raids were conducted in conjunction with heightened Iraqi police patrols.

Despite the tactical successes of these sweeps, top American commanders grasped that the task in Iraq was more than a mopping up of the remnants of Saddam's regime, that indeed the structure of Saddam's power was broader than anyone had anticipated, with deep roots in the Sunni clans and their tribal homelands north and west of Baghdad. U.S. forces were engaged in a full-blown counterinsurgency campaign, the largest such effort since the Vietnam War. While the situation in the southern Shi'a regions and in the Kurdish north of Iraq was far more peaceful and positive about the toppling of Saddam and the new Iraq to come, collapsing the Sunni Triangle would be a bigger challenge. And, as always, the strength of international terrorist organizations was difficult to judge; Iraq's borders were essentially wide open, particularly to Iran and Syria.

The June 25, 2003, testimony of General John Abizaid, nominated to replace Franks at the head of U.S. Central Command, captures well the thinking of the moment. "We are certainly in for some difficult days ahead periodically," he told the Senate Armed Services Committee. "We shouldn't kid ourselves about the fact that we can be the subject of terrorist attacks in Iraq, because we know people are coming our way."[9] Abizaid identified three sets of enemies: foreign fighters, Saddam loyalists, and common criminals exploiting the situation for their own purposes.

The reality of the counterinsurgency was also playing havoc with the Pentagon's plan to draw down U.S. forces quickly in Iraq. The original scheme had called for a reduction to two army divisions by the fall, but in light of the continuing guerrilla war, this was no longer feasible. "For the foreseeable future," reported Abizaid, "we will require a large number of troops for Iraq." The need for troop strength was in part driven by the desire to maintain the offensive drive that the sweeps represented. "They need to go out and seek the enemy, they need to bring the fight to the enemy and they need to defeat the enemy," Abizaid said of his troops. "We need to be . . . firm that we cannot be driven out," casualties notwithstanding.[10]

Skeptics of the Bush administration's Iraq policy, silenced by the rapid conquest of Baghdad and the defeat of Saddam's conventional forces, saw disasters looming in the counterinsurgency. "I thought we were holding our own until this week, and now I'm not so sure," said Richard Atchison, a retired air force intelligence officer, on June 27. "If we don't get this operation moving soon, the opposition will continue to grow, and we will have a much larger problem."[11] Laurence Pope, a retired State Department Arabist and former political adviser to CENTCOM, was in full Middle-East-cycle-of-violence mode: "Over the next months, I expect a vicious cycle in which force-protection measures will alienate the population and create more opposition, with rising casualties," he told Thomas Ricks of the *Washington Post*.[12] Indeed, commentators seemed to be fighting an entire series of past wars through Iraq. "The longer this goes on, the more violent these events will become," said retired Marine General Carlton Fulford. "We learned this in Lebanon and Somalia—and Iraq is much more challenging than either of these."[13]

As members of Congress traveled to Iraq to conduct what they had hoped would be postwar congratulatory tours, they began to voice uncertainty about the future. Democrats repeated their criticisms of the "unilateralism" of the Bush Doctrine. "Our troops are stretched very, very thin," reported Michigan Senator Carl Levin.[14]

The prospect of an extended counterinsurgency mission also soon provoked comparisons to Vietnam and the inevitability of failure. "The

Americans learned it the hard way in Vietnam," wrote Tom Lasseter of Knight Ridder Newspapers, "the Russians in Afghanistan, the British in Northern Ireland and now, it seems, the same scenario may be unfolding in Iraq." He forecast that Iraqis would unite against their occupiers, inspiring the coalition to heavier repression. "The harder an occupying force pounds back, the more it alienates the populace, creating communities that accept, if not actively support, armed resistance."[15]

The escalating violence clearly caught the Bush administration and the Pentagon off guard, and neither had an immediately coherent strategy in response. Deputy Defense Secretary Paul Wolfowitz correctly argued that the situation across Iraq was both more complex and far better than the headlines and pundits suggested. "The direction is pretty clear," he said. "It is toward a more secure Iraq. I think that the basic approach that the military is using is a sound approach." Wolfowitz also was more insightful about the underlying strategic weakness of the insurgents. "They lack the sympathy of the population, and they lack any serious external support. Basically, they're on their own."[16] Indeed, even to this date, the Sunni rejectionists have had no political leader or party to rally around, other than Saddam Hussein.

At the same time, Defense Secretary Rumsfeld was initially reluctant to acknowledge that the postcombat campaign even existed. He was particularly truculent on the question of troop strength, although he knew that his plans to reduce the U.S. force in Iraq were in tatters.

By the beginning of July, coalition commanders were bracing for increased attacks, as important Ba'ath Party annual days approached: July 14 had been the date of the 1958 coup against the monarchy, July 16 was the date that Saddam himself had come to power in 1979, and July 17 was the anniversary of the Ba'ath Party revolution in 1968. To preempt unrest, a second series of large-scale sweeps was ordered. On July 12, 2003, Operation Soda Mountain, centered in the Sunni Triangle but with raids taking place across Iraq, began. By its conclusion on July 17, the operation had encompassed more than 140 sweeps, with 611 Iraqis detained, including sixty-two former regime officials, and thousands of weapons discovered.[17] These actions were having a cumulative impact. "The effect of all these operations was that walk-in [human intelligence] doubled from early June to mid-July," said one military officer. The intelligence was "very good quality."[18]

The Bush administration also started to accelerate and expand the training of various Iraqi security forces. The immediate purpose was not simply to relieve the pressure on coalition forces, but to "put an Iraqi face" on reconstruction, as Lieutenant General Ricardo Sanchez, commander of the coalition joint task force, put it.[19] Members of the newly formed Iraqi Governing Council advocated militia units to fight the insurgency, as many factions, especially among the Shi'a and Kurdish communities, maintained their own private armed forces. The coalition thus belatedly decided to establish an Iraqi Civil Defense Corps (ICDC), separate from the new Iraqi army. These units would be raised within forty-five days and train and work with U.S. units around the country. Then the Iraqis would be stationed around fixed sites, freeing coalition forces to conduct greater offensives against the insurgents.

But well before the Iraqi militia could take the field, U.S. forces in Mosul scored a major victory when on July 23, Special Forces and units from the 101st Airborne Division surrounded and, in the ensuing gun battle, killed Saddam Hussein's two sons, Uday and Qusay. While Saddam himself remained at large and attacks on coalition forces continued, Ambassador L. Paul Bremer, head of the civilian Coalition Provisional Authority, saw the operation as a sign of improved intelligence. "We've seen an increase in informants coming forward to our military, to our intelligence people and to our police in the last three weeks, and this is an obvious example of that," he said.[20]

At the time, it was unclear what effect the death of Saddam's sons would have on the insurgency. Many Iraqis initially doubted that Uday and Qusay were indeed dead, and, despite or because of the sons' feared reputation among Iraqis, many observers were skeptical about the impact of their removal. The comments of Judith Yaphe, an Iraq specialist at the National Defense University in Washington, were typical. Acknowledging that the sons' deaths might "weaken" the resistance, she averred that the news "is not going to stop all of the attacks against us."[21]

Yet in retrospect, it is clear that the pattern of insurgent operations underwent a marked change in the wake of the large-scale sweeps and the killing of Uday and Qusay. As will be discussed below, the rejectionists began to attack "soft," or civilian, targets more frequently. And those attacks aimed at U.S. and coalition forces became more sophisticated and precise.

While the combination of Saddamists, terrorists, and common criminals would continue to take their toll among Americans, their ability to inhibit the aggressiveness of coalition operations was proving to be limited.

At the same time, Defense Secretary Rumsfeld was pressuring his lieutenants to accelerate and refine counterinsurgency tactics. In early October, Rumsfeld distributed a memo pushing for a better understanding of the "metrics" of success in a global war on terrorism and in Iraq. Although eventual press coverage tended to see a defeatist tone in the memo—in which Rumsfeld admitted that victory in Afghanistan and Iraq would require a "long, hard slog"—the key point of the memo was in seeking some tangible definition of victory. "We know we're killing a lot, capturing a lot, collecting arms. We just don't know yet whether that's the same as winning."[22]

But on the ground in Iraq, local commanders were beginning to feel they were winning, and, more important, they knew that their operations were producing success. Both tactical and strategic intelligence was improving—not only did coalition forces better know who the bad guys were, but also how to translate what was often fleeting intelligence into action. As they pieced together an improved intelligence picture, U.S. commanders also shifted their own pattern of operations. Iraqi mobster Latif Hamed al-Kubaishat and his gang, centered in the Sunni town of Baquba, were the targets of an operation dubbed Ivy Needle, conducted in late August. Operation Sweeney, conducted in October on the al Faw Pensinsula near the southern port town of Basra, targeted smugglers. CENTCOM commander Abizaid also was sensitive to the complaints of Iraqi civilians that the sweeps were netting many innocent Iraqis as well as Ba'athists and criminals. "We have to be as precise in our combat operations with ground troops going into villages as we were in our combat operations in the war," he told the New York Times. "We can't be indiscriminate. We can't just round up people and then sort them out. It makes no sense to conduct a military operation that creates more enemies than friends."[23]

Indeed, outside the Sunni Triangle, such tactics had long been standard operating procedure. In Mosul—the largest city in northern Iraq, on the southern edge of the Kurdish region and with a roughly equal mix of Sunni and Shi'a Arabs and Kurds—civic action often took priority over direct counterinsurgency operations. Major General David Petraeus, commander of the 101st Airborne with responsibility for the city and the surrounding region, often hectored his subordinates at nightly briefings to accelerate spending on public works and similar efforts. "My main weapon is dollars," he said. Similarly, in the region around Karbala and in the predominantly Shi'a south, marine units had been able to develop a much closer relationship with local leaders. The introduction of such tactics in the Sunni zone marked the progress that the sweeps had reaped.

Ironically, even as the coalition counterinsurgency campaign entered a new phase, the Iraqi resistance managed to attack successfully a number of U.S. helicopters, causing the casualty totals to spike upward. Even in retrospect, the tactical explanation for the successes is unclear, for the guerrillas had been shooting at choppers for months previously. But when a CH-47D Chinook helicopter was downed on November 2, killing sixteen soldiers, U.S. officials admitted that, of the 5,000 shoulder-launched antiaircraft missiles estimated to have been held by the Iraqi army, just one third had been accounted for or recovered, and the scope of the threat became an issue, at least for the media.[24] Nor was the danger confined to helicopters; U.S. transport aircraft arriving and departing from the Baghdad airport had occasionally been shot at and had long been using evasive maneuvers during takeoffs and landings.

In addition to the antiaircraft missiles, rocket-propelled grenades—the cheap, ubiquitous "RPG" almost as common as an AK-47 rifle—were threatening to low-flying, infantry-carrying helicopters. Although RPGs are notoriously inaccurate, they had been the munitions used during the "Black Hawk Down" attacks in Somalia in 1993, and on November 7, 2003, an American Black Hawk was hit near Tikrit. The helicopter crashed, killing six soldiers.

At the same time, the insurgents improvised other, even more headline-grabbing attacks. The first was on the al Rashid Hotel in Baghdad, while Deputy Defense Secretary Paul Wolfowitz and an entourage of American journalists were staying there. Hiding a small artillery rocket launcher in a blue trailer just outside the so-called "Green Zone" compound that makes up the coalition headquarters in Baghdad, the guerrillas remotely launched more than two dozen rockets at the hotel façade. Many of the French-made rockets misfired, most missed the target entirely, and only six exploded—but the attacks killed a U.S. Army officer in the Wolfowitz party.

On November 12, a car bomb exploded in Nasiriyah, killing eighteen Italian soldiers and more than a dozen Iraqi civilians. The attacks, the suicide tactics, and the fact that Nasiriyah is a heavily Shi'ite city shifted the public spotlight onto the threat of al Qaeda–like terrorists. Touring the site of the attack, Italian Defense Minister Antonio Martino told Italian television that his government had "some fairly reliable intelligence information" that the bombing was the work of "re-grouped al Qaeda terrorists" and Saddam fedayeen. The attacks also spooked the Japanese government, which was due to deploy forces to the vicinity. "We have consistently felt that we would like to participate in the reconstruction of Iraq as soon as possible," said Japanese spokesman Yasuo Fukuda, "but we have to consider the changing situation and respond accordingly."[25]

The Bush administration seemed to be on the defensive. In a press conference, General Abizaid dismissed the terrorist attack as far less significant than those of the former regime loyalists; he estimated the number of foreign fighters at 5,000 or fewer. The president also announced plans to accelerate plans to hand over greater security duties to the Iraqis themselves. Seemingly sensitive to the spike in casualties in Iraq, the White House again emphasized plans to "put an Iraqi face" on its reconstruction efforts.

But the headlines obscured the fundamental shift in counterinsurgency tactics and the broader success of the campaign. The volume of attacks, which had peaked at approximately forty-five per day in the early fall, had dropped to about thirty-five per day and, as Ambassador Bremer noted, were increasingly targeted not at coalition forces but at "innocent Iraqis in an effort to drive them away from the goal they share with the coalition— a democratic and peaceful Iraq."[26] Improved intelligence gave a new edge to military operations, particularly in the Sunni heartland. On November 16, the Fourth Infantry Division cordoned off the town of Auja, Saddam Hussein's birthplace, with concertina wire, issued identification cards to all male residents, and began to control closely access to what the *Washington Post* described as a "wealthy enclave of Hussein relatives on the outskirts of Tikrit."[27] Reporter Vernon Loeb characterized the operation as a "reverse strategic hamlet," contrasting the isolation of Auja with the Vietnam-era effort; this was a move to keep insurgents in, not keep them out. He quoted the infantry battalion commander in charge, Lieutenant Colonel

Steve Russell: "The insurgents should not be allowed to swim among the population as a whole," said Russell. "What we elected to do was make Auja a fishbowl so we could see who was swimming inside."[28]

These tactics underscored the key emerging fact that the insurgency was proving neither to be a politically motivated drive to restore the Ba'ath Party, nor a popularly based Sunni ethnic uprising. In Auja and the nearby town of Abu Hishma, the locals were angry, but their confinement did not seem to spark any wider unrest, even in the Sunni Triangle. Even public pandering did not work. "I see no difference between us and the Palestinians," one resident told the *New York Times*. Reporter Dexter Filkins heard an "echo of the Israeli counterinsurgency campaign in the occupied territories," but also acknowledged General Sanchez' report that the pace of insurgent attacks had been further reduced, to fewer than twenty per day.[29] Coalition forces were quite clearly beginning to preempt insurgent attacks against them.

Coalition forces were beginning not only to preempt attacks, but also to forestall future attacks by choking off guerrilla financing and arms supplies; indeed, many anticoalition strikes had been the result of direct payments from Saddam loyalists to unemployed former soldiers. "For the first time in the last 30 days, I truly feel we've gotten into their cycle of financing," Fourth Infantry Division commander Major General Ray Odierno declared on December 13. "We have indications they're having trouble financing attacks. There are indications that for the first time, they're having trouble getting their hands on weapons." The frequency of attacks had dropped to six per day and the "contract price" to kill an American soldier had jumped to $3,000, about fifteen times the price in the late summer and early fall.[30]

That same day, Odierno's troops provided the external security for the operation that punctuated the campaign: the capture of Saddam Hussein near the town of Adwar, about fifteen miles from Tikrit. U.S. soldiers found the former dictator hiding in a hole at a local farm, living an underground existence that starkly contrasted with his palaces. Powerful images of Saddam being checked for lice by an army doctor captured the psychological impact of his capture. As a battalion commander in the 101st Airborne put it, "The Wicked Witch is dead."[31]

Yet the importance of immeasurable political factors in a counterinsurgency war left many experts scrambling to assess the value of Saddam's capture. Expectations that the insurgency would collapse completely were, of course, misplaced. But those who had been trained to see the patterns of Saddam's Iraq had difficulty imagining any discontinuity. Retired Colonel Walter P. Lang, head of the Middle East section of the Defense Intelligence Agency during the Gulf War of 1991 and a frequent commentator on Operation Iraqi Freedom, argued that Saddam's apprehension "is not as profound as the administration is claiming it will be. He has not been running the war, and the war is also the product of the Sunni Arabs' unhappiness about restructuring the society in a way that will end up with the Shi'a running Iraq."[32]

Although Saddam had not been in operational command of the insurgency, his capture, which also netted a detailed organizational chart of the resistance structure, was a further intelligence coup. A focus on the cellular structure of the insurgency had helped lead to Saddam's capture, and in turn the capture gave additional insights into the cells. "What we've done in the last 60 days is really take them down," one military official explained. "We've dismantled the Baghdad piece. We've dismantled the Mosul piece. I'm not saying we've taken down the [Sunni Triangle] piece, but we've hammered it."[33] Major General Odierno believed that the insurgents had been "brought to their knees" and attacks on Americans reduced to a "fractured, sporadic threat."[34]

Analysts also missed the biggest impact of Saddam's capture—the impact on American public opinion and on the belief that the reconstruction of Iraq ultimately would succeed. As much as any single factor, the claim that the capture did not leave the United States any safer killed the presidential campaign of former Vermont Governor Howard Dean, punctuating his rapid fall from front-runner to failure. Snatching Saddam also convinced the Middle East and the rest of the world that the coalition counterinsurgency campaign reflected an American commitment to stay the course in Iraq—as did the Bush administration's announcement of a second rotation of forces, 110,000 fresh troops to replace the 125,000 that had been in Iraq for a year—in ways that the creeping tactical improvements of the previous months could not. This was a lesson that the insurgents themselves had, over the same period of time, come quite clearly to understand: When you can't kill enough Americans, try killing Iraqis and those representatives of the international community with enough courage to work for the future of Iraq.

The War That Hasn't Happened

If the United States, its forces, and its allies could not be defeated directly, it might have been possible—and still might be—to defeat the coalition indirectly by frustrating the progress of post-Saddam politics in Iraq. American leaders had long advertised their biggest fear: that, absent a dictatorial strongman of the Saddam variety, Iraq would prove ungovernable and descend into factional civil war. The Middle East's Sunni-dominated governments, not least the Saudi royal family, agreed with the U.S. foreign policy establishment that there was much to fear from a democratic Iraq likely to be dominated by the Shi'a majority. Finally, the United Nations and other international actors in Iraq made attractive targets to rejectionists failing to achieve their initial objective.

Thus as American commanders were beginning to get a better handle on the Iraqi insurgency, the guerrillas started to switch their tactics. This phase of the insurgency began on August 7 in Baghdad, when the embassy of Jordan—officially opposed to the invasion of Iraq but a longtime U.S. ally in the region—was targeted by a car bomb that killed eleven. Two weeks later, a larger bomb exploded outside the United Nations headquarters in Baghdad, killing seventeen UN officials, including Sergio Vieira de Mello, the top representative and a figure close to UN Secretary-General Kofi Annan. The bombing came as the UN had begun to play a larger role in Iraqi reconstruction, and Vieira de Mello had led Annan's effort to restore the organization's credibility and relevance following the war, by getting the Security Council to accept the legitimacy of the Iraqi Governing Council. Annan's subsequent decision to withdraw UN personnel from Baghdad was a blow to the reconstruction effort and a victory for Osama bin Laden, who had challenged the UN's traditional neutrality by declaring it "nothing but a tool of crime."[35]

Later in the month, the campaign against "neutrals" expanded with an attack on the headquarters of the International Committee of the Red Cross. Coming October 27, the first day of the Muslim holy month of Ramadan, this attack was coordinated with three attacks on Iraqi police stations. In all, thirty-five people were killed.

The larger attempt to foment civil war in Iraq began on August 30, 2003, when Ayatollah Mohammed Bakir Hakim, a member of one of Iraq's most prominent clerical families, a Shi'a who "combined political acumen with religious pedigree," and, most important, a voice for moderation in post-Saddam Iraq, was killed, along with scores of followers, in a terrorist car bomb.[36] The attack hit the Imam Ali shrine in the city of Najaf, one of the holiest Shi'a sites. A fourth initial attack, on the Baghdad headquarters of the new Iraqi police, made clear that, in the minds of the insurgents, any "collaboration" in Iraqi reconstruction—even the simple keeping of public order—was to be regarded as a hostile act.

The Iraqi Governing Council was next on the target list, when on October 12, a white Toyota Corolla sped past a Baghdad checkpoint into the parking lot of the Baghdad Hotel, often used by the council and many Americans. Although an expanded security perimeter limited the damage to the hotel, six Iraqi security guards were killed. The size of the bomb was also a warning: "There was a very big explosion," said a nearby Baghdad shopkeeper. "At the same moment I saw a car flying into the air with a big column of fire and smoke."[37]

On October 14, just after the Turkish parliament had voted to send troops to help secure the reconstruction of Iraq, another car bomb was detonated outside the Turkish embassy in Baghdad. And a day later, yet another bomb ripped through the streets of "Saddam City"—the Shi'a slum in Baghdad.[38]

These bombings, which coincided with the rocket attack on the al Rashid Hotel, again brought Vietnam analogies, particularly the 1968 Tet Offensive, to the fore. "Like Tet 1968 in Vietnam," retired Air Force Colonel Sam Gardiner told the Washington Post, "[Ramadan] is a religious holiday that is being used to show us the extent of the strength of the bad guys. Seems to me this is the first time we have seen a strategy emerge from the bad guys."[39] Said retired Marine Lieutenant General Paul van Riper, a Gulf War commander: "As has often been noted, U.S. forces fought and won a long series of battles and engagements in Vietnam—in the military sense—but lost the war. The real question today is whether the administration can articulate what its overall strategy is in Iraq, and if it can—which I seriously doubt—does the military have a campaign to carry out that strategy?"[40]

But just as many analysts failed to grasp the pattern of counterinsurgency operations in Iraq, they likewise failed to discern the degree to which the attacks against Iraqis were hardening opposition to the Saddamists and outside terrorists. Most importantly, the strategy of attacking Iraqis supporting reconstruction backfired almost from the start. In particular, the Shi'a and Kurdish leadership reacted with a deeper commitment to cooperation, both with one another and with the American-led coalition.

This stolidity has continued in 2004 in the face of increasingly spectacular attacks. On February 1, suicide bombers killed fifty-six and wounded 200 in the Kurdish-majority city of Irbil, attacking the headquarters of Kurdish political parties during a religious holiday. And on March 2, bombs exploded in Karbala and Baghdad, killing almost 200 people, as Shi'a pilgrims gathered to mark Ashura, the holiest day of the Shi'a religious year. These attacks were thought to be part of the "sectarian war" described by al Qaeda associate Abu Musab al-Zarqawi. At the same time, General Abizaid averred that coalition intelligence and Iraqi police had thwarted equally large attacks planned on Basra, the Shi'a city in the far south where a car packed with 550 pounds of explosives and a remote detonator were found at a gas station, and Kirkuk in the north, where police defused a large bomb planted beside the route of a planned Shi'a march.[41]

The attacks prompted Iraq's Shi'a, in particular, to organize protest marches and increased calls to form sectarian militias. Yet, to a large degree, these events have served admirably to vent the factions' frustrations while renewing their determination to avoid a civil war. Grand Ayatollah Ali al Sistani, the most revered Shi'a cleric, has proved to be a shrewd negotiator for his community's interests, successfully pressing for the direct elections that will almost certainly bring a Shi'a-led government, yet at the same time willing to compromise on a preconstitutional basic law that will allow for the transfer of Iraqi sovereignty from Bremer's occupation authority and reassure minorities—and even Iraqi women—that their political rights will be respected. And as violence has continued, even Sunni clerics are increasingly speaking out against the insurgents.

In sum, the resistance has had little to show for months of violence. The "sea" of the Iraqi people is drying up for the insurgents, and the effort to spark a civil war has failed as fully as the effort to attack American political will. The guerrillas' lone success has been with the "international community." Yet even here, the record is no more than mixed. Although Spain has retreated from the courageous stands taken by former Prime Minister Jose Maria Aznar, Kofi Annan is making a serious effort to find a useful role in

Iraq for the UN. And despite the periodic and tragic attacks on Iraqi police and common people, Operation Iraqi Freedom—the postcombat stability operations as well as the war itself—has created a new opportunity that Iraqis seem determined to wrench from the dying grasp of their past.

PART V

Iraqi Freedom: An Assessment

It is commonly said that the terrorist attacks of September 11, 2001, "changed the world." In fact, it has been the American reaction to the attacks, and in particular the war in Iraq, that is changing the world. President Bush's decisions to make the Middle East the centerpiece of U.S. national security policy and to insist upon a long-term strategy of promoting democracy—reversing decades of maintaining an increasingly volatile balance of regional power—mark a fundamental fork in the course of international politics. They also give purpose to the exercise of American power. As President Bush remarked in his speech before the National Endowment for Democracy in November 2003:

> Sixty years of Western nations excusing and accommodating the lack of freedom in the Middle East did nothing to make us safe— because in the long run, stability cannot be purchased at the expense of liberty. As long as the Middle East remains a place where freedom does not flourish, it will remain a place of stagnation, resentment, and violence ready for export. And with the spread of weapons that can bring catastrophic harm to our country and our friends, it would be reckless to accept the status quo.[1]

Politics, Not as Usual

When the president recognized the 9/11 attacks as an act of war demanding a military response and not just a crime to be answered by law enforcement, he propelled the United States and the world out of the "post–Cold

103

War era" that marked the 1990s and shaped the policies of the Clinton administration. During this long decade, U.S. global primacy became a recognized fact of international politics—it was in the late 1990s that French leaders began to speak of American "hyperpower"—but one which had only marginal consequences for the shape of the world. President Clinton was reluctant to leverage American might in any potentially provocative way. He was late to involve the United States in the vicious wars emanating from the collapse of Yugoslavia or to react to the increasing boldness of Chinese military intimidation of Taiwan, while North Korea was appeased through the Agreed Framework of 1994. Many of Clinton's international initiatives were either symbolic—as in his 1998 trip to Africa—or fruitless—his failure to broker an Israeli-Palestinian peace—or both—as in Northern Ireland. Even the expansion of NATO, a move of genuine significance, was protracted, and the truly challenging part, the integration of postcommunist states in southeastern Europe, was ultimately left to the Bush administration.

Most importantly, the Clinton administration was reluctant to deploy American power in the Middle East. President Clinton encouraged the belief that the region's problems could be dealt with through a concert of the traditional "great powers" acting under the aegis of the United Nations. It is no coincidence that those nations who object most strenuously to the policies of the Bush administration in the Middle East—notably France, Germany, Russia, and China—yearn for the hands-off attitude of the Clinton years. The Clinton administration also reinforced the fantasy that solving the Israeli-Palestinian conflict was the strategic key to the region—and that it could be solved without mention of the dysfunctional political dynamic of most states in the region.

Bush's vision for the democratization of the Middle East will be the shaping reality of international politics for decades to come. Operation Iraqi Freedom gives substance to the doctrine, demonstrating that the United States is willing to topple tyrannical states as well as terror organizations like al Qaeda. It is an extraordinarily ambitious undertaking, and the outcome is uncertain. Moreover, there have been and will continue to be tremendous costs: in lives, in treasure, and in opportunities lost elsewhere. As is becoming ever more apparent, the Bush administration is betting that rising Chinese power will not have immediately violent consequences.

Yet the invasions of Iraq and Afghanistan have undeniably created new facts in the greater Middle East. The region's governments have grasped that the status quo is changing: Libya's Muammar Gaddafi, once described by President Ronald Reagan as the "mad dog of the Middle East," is trying to reinvent himself as an economic reformer, a capitalist autocrat in something of the manner of China's Deng Tsiao-Ping. Gaddafi's apparent decision to surrender his WMD programs is an offering to appease an America he says he fears.

Troublingly, however, today's international institutions remain ill suited to support or implement the Bush Doctrine. Just as the United Nations failed to address the problem of Saddam Hussein's murderous regime, it is likewise unprepared to promote the democratization of the greater Middle East, particularly when much of the problem stems from its own member states. The NATO alliance is striving admirably to adapt to changing geopolitical circumstances and to develop forces more useful to the war on terrorism, but as long as France and Germany remain opposed to American policy, these reform efforts are likely to have a limited effect.

At the same time, those nations most opposed to the American-led mission in the Middle East seem to have little ability to act directly against the United States. Some observers argue that France and others are employing "soft power" to thwart American purposes in the Middle East.[2] By ensnaring the administration in the disarmament dead-end in the United Nations, for instance, Paris drove a wedge between America and the world, "softly balancing" what they could not otherwise influence.

Unfortunately for the theory of soft power, the French exercise had little appreciable balancing effect. French maneuvering did not induce the Bush administration to want to do what Jacques Chirac wished it to do—leave Saddam Hussein in power—or to acquiesce to Dominique de Villepin's desires. France's vision of a multipolar world order holds little attraction for Americans and is unlikely to entice anyone outside the McGovern wing of the Democratic Party to imitate it.

Indeed, Russia and China, the other two members of the Security Council's Axis of Veto, were quick to distance themselves from the French folly. Russian President Vladimir Putin expressed his regrets to President Bush about the U.S. decision to remove Saddam, but emphasized that there was no irreparable damage to relations. Like Boris Yeltsin before

him, Putin essentially shrugged at American actions he did not care for—
as with NATO expansion, the ABM Treaty, and the wars in the Balkans,
the Russian objections to getting rid of Saddam and the Ba'ath Party were
not serious enough to provoke an enduring split with the United States.
Putin understands that the return to great power will be a long road, and
his first purpose is to make Russia prosper economically. Even should
Russia wish to oppose America again in the future, a premature attempt
to do so would abort the effort.

Like Putin, Hu Jintao is probably breathing a huge sigh of relief that
President Bush did not demand a vote at the UN; it was one thing to stand
near while France brandished its UN veto, quite another to have had to
"lay its card upon the table" had Bush forced the issue. Chinese strategists
find their game plan for patiently accumulating great power entirely overcome by events since September 11—everywhere they turn, they see new
American outposts. Beijing has become more cautious as the Bush administration has asserted its global leadership.

Even Germans, their genuine revulsion from violence and war cyni-
cally exploited by Gerhard Schroeder, are awaking with morning-after
regrets. The prospect of abandonment by the Americans, or even the
"repositioning" of the U.S. garrison in Germany to the east, is frightening;
following France has been a disaster that threatens the union of Europe
that was safely to bind Germany to the rest of the continent.

At the same time that America's opponents lack the ability or the
willpower to block its initiatives in the Middle East, their lack of support
is problematic. At the moment, but for the help of Great Britain, Australia,
newly free nations of Eastern Europe, and traditional allies in East Asia,
like Japan and South Korea, most of the world has yet to commit itself to
creating a new order in Iraq or the region.

The ultimate success or failure of the American project in Iraq will
mark a defining moment in international politics. Success there—measured
by the creation and continued nurturing of a genuinely representative and
increasingly liberal democracy—will not only create new political possi-
bilities in the Arab Middle East but affirm direct American presence in the
region; there will no longer be any doubt that the Persian Gulf and the
surrounding areas lie within the U.S. "security perimeter." Conversely,
failure in Iraq—measured by the renewed acceptance of the region's

largely despotic and corrupt governments—will not only foreclose the future of freedom but also excite a new competition for power. And that is certain to lead to increased terrorism, targeted at Americans abroad and at home, with an increased risk that these attacks will employ chemical, biological, radiological, or nuclear weapons.

President Bush's strong assertion of American international leadership and determination to reorder the Middle East have also transformed U.S. domestic politics. While the outcome of the 2000 elections left many Democrats doubting the legitimacy of the president, the war in Iraq sharpened the partisan lines. The presidential candidacy of former Vermont Governor Howard Dean was, in some essential ways, incomprehensible but for the war. The Dean campaign also has had an undeniable impact upon the Democratic Party, forcing Senator John Kerry to recant even his hedged support for the war. The 2004 campaign will be in some measure a referendum on Iraq and, for the first time since the end of the Cold War, Americans will be voting to choose a "wartime" president.

A Doctrine in Search of a Strategy

Even as the Bush Doctrine has reordered international and domestic politics, it is an incomplete strategy—a strategy in the making. While the September 2002 *National Security Strategy* defined clearly, even elegantly, the purposes of American power, it is far less clear as to how the stated goals, "political and economic freedom, peaceful relations with other states, and respect for human dignity," are to be achieved.[3] Setting national security priorities is the central task of any strategy, if it is to provide guidance to policymaking, military planning, programming, or budgeting. The priorities of the Bush Doctrine are being defined *a posteriori* and primarily by Operation Iraqi Freedom and the continuing American commitment in the region.

The Bush Doctrine contains within in it several layers of strategic choice. The first is that the anti-American and anti-Western violence that stems from instability in the greater Middle East is the most pressing danger to the international, liberal order. A second is that, within the region—the "Islamic world" that stretches from West Africa to East Asia—the problems of the Arab heartland should be addressed first. A third and final choice is that, within the Arab heartland—itself a tremendous swath of territory—Iraq is the top priority.

President Bush's May 1, 2003, speech aboard the USS *Abraham Lincoln*, marking the conclusion of "major combat operations" in Operation Iraqi Freedom, widely caricatured as a swaggering triumph, is in fact a speech that strikes somber notes, defining ultimate success as achievable but certainly distant, requiring great resolve to reach. "The battle of Iraq is one victory in a war on terror that began on September 11, 2001—and still goes on," said Bush.

> Our mission continues. Al Qaeda is wounded, not destroyed. The scattered cells of the terrorist network still operate in many nations, and we know from daily intelligence that they continue to plot against free people. The proliferation of deadly weapons remains a serious danger. The enemies of freedom are not idle, and neither are we. Our government has taken unprecedented measure to defend the homeland. And we will continue to hunt down the enemy before he can strike.
>
> The war on terror is not over; yet it is not endless. We do not know the day of final victory, but we have seen a turning of the tide. No act of the terrorists will change our purpose, or weaken our resolve, or alter their fate. Their cause is lost. Free nations will press on to victory.[4]

The victory the president seeks is not meant as a more robust version of the containment of the past, but rather a wholesale transformation of the Middle Eastern political order. As the challenges of postwar Iraq have become plainer, the administration has spoken more clearly about the immensity of the task of the global war on terrorism: "a generational commitment," in the words of National Security Adviser Condoleezza Rice, "to helping the people of the Middle East transform their region." Dr. Rice drew an extended analogy between the reconstruction of post-Saddam Iraq and post-Nazi Europe:

> Like the transformation of Europe, the transformation of the Middle East will require a commitment of many years. . . .

America and our friends and allies must engage broadly throughout the region, across many fronts, including diplomatic, economic and cultural [fronts]. And—as in Europe—our efforts must work in full partnership with the peoples of the region who share our commitment to human freedom and who see it in their own self-interest to defend that commitment.

And we must have the perseverance to see it through. There is an understandable tendency to look back on America's experience in post-war Germany and see only the successes. But the road we traveled was very difficult. [The years] 1945 through 1947 were especially challenging. The Marshall Plan was actually a response to the failed efforts to rebuild Germany in late '45 and early '46. SS officers—called "werewolves"—attacked coalition forces and engaged in sabotage, much like today's Baathist and fedayeen remnants.[5]

Any lingering doubts about U.S. strategic priorities evaporated with President Bush's September 7, 2003, address calling for a huge increase in military operational and reconstruction funds for Iraq. He reminded "the Congress and the country that the war on terror would be a lengthy war, a different kind of war, fought on many fronts in many places." But, the president argued:

Iraq is now the central front. Enemies of freedom are making a desperate stand there—and there they must be defeated. This will take time and require sacrifice. Yet we will do what is necessary, we will spend what is necessary, to achieve this essential victory in the war on terror, to promote freedom and to make our own nation more secure.[6]

Perhaps no other statement better characterizes the transformation of U.S. national security strategy since the Cold War. In 1989, the Soviet Union was the enemy, and the German plain was the central front; now, terrorists and the states that foster them are the enemy, and the flood plains of Mesopotamia are the central front. Also unlike the Cold War, American strategy today is primarily offensive. "We have carried the fight to the enemy," said the president on September 7. "We are rolling back the terrorist threat to civilization, not on the fringes of its influence, but at the heart of its power."[7]

But if President Bush has not lost his eloquence in expressing his strategic purposes, neither has he found a way to instill the institutions of American power with an equal sense of urgency or commitment. The president seems the inverse of his father. Where Bush *père* admitted to a lack of vision, his son has a stunning dream of a transformed Middle East. George H. W. Bush was the great helmsman at the wheel of the American ship of state; George W. Bush plots a bold course and leaves it to the crew to work the rudder. The loose connections among the White House, the Pentagon, the State Department, and the intelligence community hampered prewar diplomacy and military planning, but they did not have immediately fatal consequences. But as the war in Iraq moves farther from the period of major combat operations and into a counterinsurgency campaign, the measures of victory shift.

The administration's internal squabbles are especially debilitating in light of the continued challenge of securing meaningful international cooperation. Given the deep fear of radical change that animated the anti-American opposition during the prewar debate generally and particularly in the United Nations process, it is likely to be some time before there is sufficient change of heart or sufficient commitment of resources to the reconstruction of Iraq among those who did not fight the war in the first place.

The Bush administration mostly has been quite clear-eyed about the prospects for so-called "internationalization" of the mission in Iraq, even as it makes good-faith efforts to try to enlist new partners. Moreover, what genuine military contribution such a coalition might make is far from clear. But where the administration is realistic about internationalization, it retains unrealistic hopes for "Iraqification"—particularly insofar as it intends to turn security matters over to a reconstructed Iraqi government. While the Bush administration is rightly committed to returning control of the country to Iraqis, "Iraqification" cannot be an excuse for American retreat.

In sum, the administration is curiously reluctant to admit that the task in Iraq is, for the foreseeable future, a test for the United States. Already most Iraqis stand with us, but otherwise, but for the British and some small bands of other allies, we stand alone. We must accept that fact and adapt to it.

The most compelling strategic argument for the Bush Doctrine is that it alone, of realistically possible futures, offers the United States and the world some hope for security, liberty, and prosperity. The most compelling argument against the doctrine is that it calls for disproportionate sacrifices, of blood and treasure, on the part of Americans and their closest allies. Operation Iraqi Freedom represented the first step in a generational commitment to Iraq, but also the commitment of many generations to transforming the greater Middle East. Paradoxically, if the administration does not clearly and relatively quickly make this adaptation in Iraq, its strategy for the Arab heartland and the Islamic world and its vision of an expanding liberal global order could well collapse. The vision of the Bush Doctrine is hugely ambitious; in embracing this great vision, the United States must obligate the resources and create the institutions necessary to realize it. This includes many aspects of the U.S. government and indeed international institutions, but most centrally it depends upon the restructuring and rebuilding of the American defense establishment.

A Spike—or the New Baseline?

There is an ongoing argument in the Pentagon about whether the current U.S. troop commitment in Iraq—138,000 soldiers—and Afghanistan—another 10,000 or so—represents an anomalous peak of activity or something like a constant level of operations. If the central tenets of this report are correct—that the primary strategic goal for the United States is to establish a new, more representative and truly stable order in the greater Middle East and that the traditional strategy of power-balancing is no longer feasible—then the answer is that the higher pace of operations is the new reality and a reasonable basis for defense planning.

This conclusion is very much at odds with today's Pentagon program as articulated in the 2001 Quadrennial Defense Review. To be fair, the review, although published after the September 11 attacks, was the product of many previous months' work. Nonetheless, Rumsfeld and his lieutenants have given no indication that they intend to revise their thinking in light of events since then. They remain strongly committed to what the QDR described as a "capabilities-based" approach to defense planning:

"This capabilities-based model focuses more on how an adversary might fight rather than on whom the adversary might be or where a war might occur."[8]

The war in Iraq—or rather, the two wars—have highlighted the short-comings of this approach. The Pentagon clearly failed to anticipate how the Iraqis would fight, or at least failed to judge the level of guerrilla resistance. Conversely, the Bush Doctrine makes it clear that the greater Middle East is where U.S. forces are most likely to be engaged. Moreover, the difficulty of suppressing the insurgency in Iraq has revealed that the American military is inadequately sized and structured for long-term constabulary missions. The heavy reliance on reserve component forces, which comprise approximately 40 percent of the second rotational force in Iraq, complicates the American ability to make the kind of "generational commitment" described by the Bush administration. While in some ways this retains a salutary effect, ensuring that military decisions engage a broader element of American society, it is also clear that the current military structures, designed for the Cold War, are flawed.

Further, Operation Iraqi Freedom will reinforce the sense in the Middle East that waging a conventional war against U.S.-led military coalitions is a losing proposition. The alternatives—terrorism and guerrilla war on the one hand, and the acquisition of weapons of mass destruction on the other hand—will have greater appeal, as Iran's behavior strongly suggests. While the region is beginning to accept that the United States will not easily be driven from Iraq and Afghanistan, those who fear greater direct American involvement—who have opposed the increasing level of involvement over the past decades—will likely hedge against and hope for the day that U.S. forces leave Iraq and the Middle East.

The overwhelming success of the initial invasion of Iraq, despite the small forces involved, both on the ground and in the air, and despite the difficulties posed by the denial of access to Turkey and the resistance of Iraqi irregulars, underscores the predominance of American conventional military power. This extraordinary ability to strike at enemy regimes and swiftly defeat, destroy, or outmaneuver enemy forces, at great distances from the United States and with limited points of access, gives the United States a tremendous advantage. But the challenges of the postinvasion operations and the need to keep U.S. troops in Iraq for the longer term underscore the brittleness of current force structure. Striking power—the ability to apply firepower—is only half the equation.

Yet the current process of defense "transformation" is intended to reinforce and extend U.S. advantages in firepower without addressing the need for additional abilities to conduct stability operations. The Pentagon leadership remains adamantly opposed to increasing the manpower strength of the armed services and especially the U.S. Army, which naturally carries the brunt of constabulary duties. Indeed, it is argued that troop strength is an anachronistic measure of military power. But stability operations are inherently manpower intensive. Until defense planners begin to account for that fact—until they accept that this level of activity is something like the new baseline—the process of defense transformation will be dangerously incomplete and it will not have reckoned with the most obvious and profound change in U.S. national security strategy.

Some experts suggest that the United States should create specialized "peacekeeping" units within the armed forces. However, this would only exacerbate the current problem. There is no "peace" to keep in the Sunni Triangle—and where conditions are more stable, such as the Kurdish north or the Shi'a south, Iraqis themselves are better suited to assume responsibility for policing. Rather, it is the flexibility of general-purpose conventional forces, their mobility and even their potential firepower, that accounts for much of the success of counterinsurgency operations thus far. Without doubt, adding specialized capabilities to the current force structure—such as more Arab linguists and civil affairs units—makes sense, but the biggest need is to be able to sustain a high level of commitment and professional performance.

While it will naturally take time and much analysis to craft the reforms and recreate the units necessary to secure the victory in Iraq, complete the victory in Afghanistan, and prepare the U.S. armed forces to sustain a generational commitment to transforming the Middle East, it is not necessary to wait until the 2005 Quadrennial Defense Review to begin to make the required changes. The real challenge is in making the political and budgetary choice to rebuild a force adequate to the missions so clearly before it.

Simply put, the goals of the Bush Doctrine cannot be secured by an American military only marginally changed from the force inherited from the Clinton years. No amount of transformational reform can bridge the gap between an expanding strategy and a shrunken force. The mismatch between ends and means is simply too great.

Notes

Prologue: The Road to Baghdad, 1991

1. This account is a summary of Thomas Donnelly, "The Road to Baghdad," *Army Times*, January 25, 1993, 1–22.

2. Ibid., 16

Part I: The Political and Strategic Setting

1. See Steve Coll, *Ghost Wars: The Secret History of the CIA, Afghanistan, and bin Laden, from the Soviet Invasion to September 10, 2001* (New York: Penguin Press, 2004), 28, 79.

2. Jimmy Carter, "State of the Union Address," January 23, 1980, http://www.this nation.com/library/sotu/1980jc.html.

3. Jennifer Huang, "A Cold War Legacy of Persian Gulf Conflict," Newsdesk.org, http://www.artsandmedia.net/cgi-bin/dc/newsdesk/2003/03/18_centcom_1?t=print.

4. Norman Kempster, "U.S. Favors Iraq in War, Shultz Indicates," *Los Angeles Times*, December 17, 1986, 22.

5. Guy Gugliotta, interview with former assistant secretary of defense Noel Koch, "At War, Iraq Courted U.S. into Economic Embrace," *Washington Post*, September 16, 1990, A34. Quoted in Douglas A. Borer, "Inverse Engagement: Lessons from U.S.-Iraq Relations, 1982–1990," *Parameters* (Summer 2003): 51–65.

6. Borer, "Inverse Engagement," 53.

7. Ibid.

8. "The Rise of Third World Threats," quoted in Michael Gordon and Bernard Trainor, *The Generals' War: The Inside Story of the Conflict in the Gulf* (Boston: Little, Brown and Co., 1995), 10.

9. NSD-26, quoted in Gordon and Trainor, *The Generals' War*, 11–12; Kenneth Pollack, *The Threatening Storm: The Case for Invading Iraq* (New York: Random House, 2002), 28.

10. Pollack, *The Threatening Storm*, 31; Gordon and Trainor, *The Generals' War*, 13.

11. Quoted in Lawrence F. Kaplan and William Kristol, *The War over Iraq* (San Francisco: Encounter Books, 2003), 42.

12. Bob Woodward, *The Commanders* (New York: Simon and Schuster, 1991), 269.

13. Colin Powell with Joseph E. Persico, *My American Journey* (New York: Random House, 1995), 470.

14. Ibid.

15. Norman Schwarzkopf with Peter Petre, *It Doesn't Take a Hero* (New York: Bantam Books, 1992), 497–98.

16. Powell, *My American Journey*, 531.

17. Ibid., 528.

18. George H. W. Bush and Brent Scowcroft, *A World Transformed* (New York: Vintage Books, 1999), 433.

19. Powell, *My American Journey*, 527.

20. Michael Gordon, "Raids on Iraq: Few Choices for Clinton," *New York Times*, January 21, 1993.

21. "Excerpts from Interview with Clinton on Goals for Presidency," *New York Times*, June 28, 1992, A17.

22. Quoted in Kaplan and Kristol, *The War over Iraq*, 50, 134.

23. William J. Clinton, quoted by Scott W. Webster, "President Bill Clinton's Foreign Policy: A Critical Assessment," Roundtable Discussion Sponsored by the Center for the Advanced Study of Leadership and the Fulbright International Center, University of Maryland, May 7, 1999.

24. William J. Clinton, "Foreign Policy Speech, San Francisco, CA," The White House, Office of the Press Secretary, February 26, 1999.

25. Martin Indyk, quoted in Pollack, *The Threatening Storm*, 66.

26. William J. Clinton, "Remarks by the President in Cabinet Meeting," The White House, Office of the Press Secretary, June 28, 1993.

27. Bradley Graham and R. Jeffrey Smith, "U.S. Aids Some Kurds, but Not Those in Anti-Saddam Group," *Washington Post*, September 10, 1996, A21.

28. Daniel Williams, "Time May Be Arch-Foe in Struggle with Iraq," *Washington Post*, December 22, 1998, A25.

29. Jocelyn Noveck, "Anger, Relief, but Little Support as Desert Fox Ends," *Associated Press*, December 20, 1998, AM Cycle.

30. George W. Bush, "A Period of Consequences," September 23, 1999, http://www.citadel.edu/pao/addreses/pres_bush.htl; George W. Bush, "A Distinctly American Internationalism," November 19, 1999, http://www.holyoke.edu/acad/intelrel/bush/wspeech.htm.

31. Bush, "A Distinctly American Internationalism."

32. Michael Gordon, "Bush Would Stop U.S. Peacekeeping in Balkan Fights," *New York Times*, October 21, 2000, A1.

33. Ibid.

34. For examples of Bush campaign rhetoric, see James Carney, "Real World Lessons in Humility," *Time.com*, June 5, 2001, http://www.time.com/time/columnist;

Tony Karon, "For Bush, Humility and the 'Global Gag Order' Don't Mix," *Time.com*, March 12, 2002, http://www.time.com/time/columnist/karon/article.

35. Rachel Post, "Our Humble Nation-Building Values," *North Gate News*, University of California Berkeley Graduate School of Journalism, October 11, 2000, http://journalism.berkeley.edu/ngn/berkeley/101100.post.html.

36. Robert Kagan, "At Last, Straight Talk on China," *Washington Post*, April 29, 2001, B07.

37. Bob Woodward, *Bush at War* (New York: Simon & Schuster, 2002), 15–20, 41; Scott Pelley, "The President's Story," *60 Minutes II*, CBS News, September 11, 2003, http://www.cbsnews.com/stories/2002/09/11/60II/main521718.shtml.

38. George W. Bush, "Address to a Joint Session of Congress and the American People," The White House, Office of the Press Secretary, September 20, 2001.

39. George W. Bush, "Remarks by the President to the Warsaw Conference on Combating Terrorism," The White House, Office of the Press Secretary, November 6, 2001.

40. Janine Zacharia, "Bush Warns Iraq on Weapons of Mass Destruction," *Jerusalem Post*, November 27, 2001, http://www.jpost.com/Editions/2001/11/27/News/News.38843.html.

41. George W. Bush, "President Delivers State of the Union Address," The White House, Office of the Press Secretary, January 29, 2002.

42. Ibid.

43. George W. Bush, "President Delivers Graduation Speech at West Point," The White House, Office of the Press Secretary, June 1, 2002.

44. Ibid.

45. George W. Bush, *The National Security Strategy of the United States* (Washington, D.C.: The White House, September 2002).

46. Ibid.

47. George W. Bush, "President's Remarks to the Nation," The White House, Office of the Press Secretary, September 11, 2002.

48. Ibid.

49. George W. Bush, "President's Remarks at the United Nations General Assembly," The White House, Office of the Press Secretary, September 12, 2002.

50. Ibid.

51. Ibid.

52. Ibid.

53. U.S. Department of State, "Senators Back President Bush on Iraq Resolution," October 2, 2002, http://usinfo.state.gov/topical/pol/arms/02100333.htm.

54. John Edwards, "Senator Edwards' Statement on Iraq Resolution," October 10, 2002, http://edwards.senate.gov/press/2002/1010a-pr.html.

55. "Senate Approves Iraq War Resolution," *CNN.com*, October 11, 2002.

56. United Nations, "UN Security Council Resolution 1441," November 8, 2002, http://www.un.org.

57. Glenn Kessler and Colum Lynch, "France Vows to Block Resolution on Iraq War," *Washington Post*, January 21, 2003, A01.

58. Ibid.

59. Colin L. Powell, "A Policy of Evasion and Deception," *Washington Post*, February 6, 2003, A24.

60. Richard Bernstein, "Speech Praised by Europe's Politicians, but Public Is Still Unpersuaded," *New York Times*, February 6, 2003, A21.

61. Richard Bernstein, "German Demonstrators Oppose War, not U.S.," *New York Times*, February 9, 2003, A14.

62. George W. Bush, "President Discusses Future of Iraq," The White House, Office of the Press Secretary, February 26, 2003.

63. Rick Atkinson, *Crusade: The Untold Story of the Persian Gulf War* (Boston: Houghton Mifflin Company, 1993), 497.

64. George W. Bush, "President Says Saddam Hussein Must Leave Iraq within 48 Hours," The White House, Office of the Press Secretary, March 17, 2003.

Part II: Military Planning

1. For fuller discussion of some aspects of the development of the war plan, see "OPLAN 1003 Major War—East," *GlobalSecurity.org*, http://www.globalsecurity.org/military/ops/oplan-1003.htm.

2. The story of this meeting has already passed from history into legend; the most detailed account is to be found in Woodward, *Bush at War*, 83–85. Other portrayals seem to be largely premised on Woodward's; for example, see Ivo H. Daalder and James M. Lindsay, *America Unbound: The Bush Revolution in Foreign Policy* (Washington, D.C.: Brookings Institution Press, 2004), 102–4.

3. Bob Woodward, *Plan of Attack* (New York: Simon & Schuster, 2004), 1–4.

4. Linda Kozaryn, "U.S. Will Combat Terrorism 'As Long As It Takes,'" *American Forces Press Service*, December 28, 2001, http://www.defenselink.mil/news/Jan2002/n01032002_200201031.html.

5. These numbers are a rough average of those publicly available and closely approximate those in Williamson Murray and Major General Robert H. Scales Jr., *The Iraq War: A Military History* (Cambridge, Mass.: The Belknap Press of Harvard University Press, 2003), 82–84. The most comprehensive description of Iraq's armed forces can be found in Anthony H. Cordesman, *The Iraq War: Strategy, Tactics, and Military Lessons* (Washington, D.C.: CSIS Press, 2003), 41–53, but this study in turn cites the International Institute for Strategic Studies and Jane's Information Group, and its estimates are, generally, somewhat higher than the figures cited here.

6. "The Strategic Defence Review: A New Chapter," UK Ministry of Defence, July 2002.

7. Ibid.

8. Peter Slevin, "Bush to Cast War as Part of Regional Strategy," *Washington Post*, February 26, 2003, A19.

9. Vernon Loeb, "Cost of War Remains Unanswered Question," *Washington Post*, March 1, 2003, A13.

10. Philip P. Pan, "U.S. Giving Up on Turks and Rerouting Ships," *Washington Post*, March 14, 2003, A01.

Part III: Major Combat Operations

1. Bob Woodward, "Attack Was 48 Hours Old When It 'Began,'" *Washington Post*, March 23, 2003, A1.

2. Ibid.

3. Murray and Scales, *The Iraq War*, 98–99.

4. Ibid., 99–100.

5. Bing West and Ray Smith, *The March Up* (New York: Bantam Books, 2003), 15.

6. For a full description of these attacks, see West and Smith, *The March Up*, 6–29.

7. The most complete account of the British efforts is to be found in Murray and Scales, *The Iraq War*, 129–53.

8. U.S. Air Force, *Operation Iraqi Freedom—By the Numbers*, April 30, 2003.

9. "Defense Secretary Donald Rumsfeld Holds News Briefing," *FDCH Political Transcripts*, March 21, 2003.

10. An excellent exposition of the marine attack into Nasiriyah can be found in West and Smith, *The March Up*, 31–48.

11. Murray and Scales, *The Iraq War*, 104.

12. Author interviews; see also Murray and Scales, *The Iraq War*, 127–28.

13. Author interviews; see also West and Smith, *The March Up*, 73–84.

14. Murray and Scales, *The Iraq War*, 171–72.

15. Ibid., 203–4.

16. Ibid., 203–6.

17. James Kitfield, "Attack Always," *National Journal*, April 26, 2003, http://www.nexis.com.

18. I Marine Expeditionary Force, *I MEF Operation Iraqi Freedom*, undated.

19. West and Smith, *The March Up*, 78.

20. I Marine Expeditionary Force, *I MEF Operation Iraqi Freedom*, undated.

21. For a fuller description of the marines' attack across the Tigris, see West and Smith, *The March Up*, 133–48.

22. See 101st Airborne Division, *101st Airborne Division (ASSLN) in Operation IRAQI FREEDOM 06 February 03–01 September 03*, undated.

23. See "Battle for al Kifl; 27 March 2003," in ibid.

24. Keith B. Richburg, "British Use Raids to Wear Down Iraqi Fighters," *Washington Post*, April 3, 2003, A25; for more on the fall of Basra, see also Murray and Scales, *The Iraq War*, 144–53.

25. Murray and Scales, *The Iraq War*, 193.

26. Sean Naylor, "Sights Set on Baghdad," *Army Times*, April 14, 2003, 15.

27. Quoted in Anthony H. Cordesman, "The Status of Iraqi Land Forces and Security/Intelligence Forces," April 10, 2003, 4, http://www.csis.org/burke/mb/iraq_statuslandforces.pdf.

28. Naylor, "Sights Set on Baghdad," 16.

29. Ibid.

30. David Zucchino, "The Thunder Run," *Los Angeles Times Magazine*, December 7, 2003, 18.

31. Murray and Scales, *The Iraq War*, 210.

32. Third Infantry Division, *Third Infantry Division (Mechanized) After Action Report: Operation IRAQI FREEDOM*, undated, p. 22.

33. Murray and Scales, *The Iraq War*, 211.

34. Araminta Wordsworth, "Comical Ali Back on TV," *National Post*, January 13, 2004, A12.

35. David Zucchino, "Iraq's Swift Defeat Blamed on Leaders," *Los Angeles Times*, August 11, 2003, 1.

36. Murray and Scales, *The Iraq War*, 212.

37. Ibid., 218. For a detailed account of the fighting along the initial supply route into Baghdad, see ibid., 212–18.

38. For a more detailed account of the marines' fighting along the Tigris outside Baghdad, see West and Smith, *The March Up*, 133–66.

39. I Marine Expeditionary Force, "Diyalah River Crossing," *I MEF Operation Iraqi Freedom* briefing.

Part IV: The Counterinsurgency Campaign

1. Daniel Williams, "U.S. Stages Raid to Quell Iraqi Attacks; Suspected Hussein Loyalists Targeted," *Washington Post*, June 12, 2003, A1.

2. U.S. Central Command, "4th Infantry Division and Task Force 'Ironhorse' Conclude Operation Peninsula Strike," Press Release 03-05-55, June 14, 2003.

3. Williams, "U.S. Stages Raid."

4. Thomas E. Ricks, "U.S. Adopts Aggressive Tactics on Iraqi Fighters; Intensified Offensive Leads to Detentions, Intelligence," *Washington Post*, July 28, 2003, A1.

5. 101st Airborne Division, private briefing with author, June 26, 2003.

6. Ibid.

7. Ibid.

8. U.S. Central Command, "Task Force Ironhorse Launches Operation Sidewinder," Press Release 03-06-96, June 29, 2003.

9. Eric Schmitt, "After the War: New Commander; Further Attacks on Allies Predicted by U.S. General," *New York Times*, June 26, 2003, A1.

10. Ibid.

11. Thomas E. Ricks, "Experts Question Depth of Victory; Attacks Indicate Ba'ath Party Is Not Cowed," *Washington Post*, June 27, 2003, A1.

12. Ibid.

13. Ibid.

14. Thomas E. Ricks and Rajiv Chandrasekaran, "In Postwar Iraq, the Battle Widens; Recent Attacks on U.S. Forces Raise Concerns of a Guerrilla Conflict," *Washington Post*, July 7, 2003, A1.

15. Tom Lasseter, "Iraqis Practice Resembles Guerrilla Warfare," *Knight Ridder Newspapers*, June 30, 2003, http://www.mercurynews.com/mld/mercurynews/news/special_packages/iraq/6205007.html.

16. Ricks, "Experts Question Depth of Victory."

17. U.S. Central Command, "Operation Soda Mountain Concludes," Press Release 03-07-56, July 18, 2003.

18. Ricks, "U.S. Adopts Aggressive Tactics on Iraqi Fighters."

19. Eric Schmitt, "U.S. Is Creating an Iraqi Militia to Relieve G.I.'s," *New York Times*, July 21, 2003, A6.

20. Eric Schmitt and Thom Shanker, "After the War: Controlling Iraq; With Hussein's Heirs Gone, Hopes Rise for End to Attacks," *New York Times*, July 23, 2003, A1.

21. Ibid.

22. Vernon Loeb, "Rumsfeld Seeks Better Intelligence on Iraqi Insurgents," *Washington Post*, December 11, 2003, A1.

23. Eric Schmitt, "After the War; Strategy; G.I.'s Shift to More Precise, Smaller Raids," *New York Times*, September 2, 2003, A1.

24. Eric Schmitt, "Attack on U.S. Copter Highlights a Constant Threat Faced by Aircraft in Iraq," *New York Times*, November 3, 2003, A1.

25. Quoted in Eric Schmitt and David E. Sanger, "The Struggle for Iraq: Guerrillas Posing More Danger, Says U.S. Commander for Iraq," *New York Times*, November 14, 2003, A1.

26. Rajiv Chandrasekaran, "General Cites Decline in Attacks on U.S. Forces; New Offensive Credited; Insurgents Shift Tactics as Result, Bremer Says," *Washington Post*, November 26, 2003, A18.

27. Vernon Loeb, "U.S. Isolates Hussein's Birthplace; Razor-Wire Fence Helps Troops Keep Tabs on Residents in Pockets of Insurgency," *Washington Post*, November 17, 2003, A14.

28. Ibid.

29. Dexter Filkins, "A Region Enflamed: Strategy; Tough New Tactics by U.S. Tighten Grip on Iraq Towns," *New York Times*, December 7, 2003, A1.

30. See Eric Schmitt, "General Says Cash and Arms Are Cut Off in Iraqi Hotbed," *New York Times,* December 13, 2003, A1.

31. Rajiv Chandrasekaran, Thomas E. Ricks, and Anthony Shadid, "Belief That Insurgency Will Fade May Be Misplaced," *Washington Post*, December 15, 2003, A1.

32. Michael R. Gordon, "The Capture of Hussein: The Insurgency; For U.S. Foes, a Major Blow: Fighters Now Lack a Symbol," *New York Times*, December 15, 2003, A1.

33. Thomas E. Ricks and Liz Spayd, "A Measure of Success in Iraq; Commanders See Signs of Progress, and New Pitfalls," *Washington Post*, January 23, 2004, A1.

34. Ibid.

35. See Colum Lynch, "U.N. Staff's Immunity from Terror Ends; Officials Say Envoy Is Most Senior Killed in Mideast since 1949," *Washington Post*, August 20, 2003, A1.

36. Anthony Shadid, "Ayatollah's Death Deepens U.S. Woes; Spiritual and Political Figure Backed Transition Effort," *Washington Post*, August 30, 2003, A1.

37. Alex Brenson, "Car Bomb Kills 6 at Baghdad Hotel, At Least 35 Hurt," *Washington Post*, October 13, 2003, A16.

38. Theola Labbe, "Car Bomb Explodes outside Turkish Embassy in Baghdad; Suicide Attack Is 3rd in Past Week against Those Allied with U.S.," *Washington Post*, October 15, 2003.

39. Vernon Loeb, "New Enemy May Require New Tactics; Non-Iraqis Now a Concern for U.S. Military Planners," *Washington Post*, October 28, 2003, A1.

40. Ibid.

41. Dexter Filkins and Eric Schmitt, "Other Attacks Averted in Iraq, General Says," *New York Times*, March 4, 2004, A1.

Part V: Iraqi Freedom: An Assessment

1. George W. Bush, "Remarks by the President at the 20th Anniversary of the National Endowment for Democracy," The White House, Office of the Press Secretary, November 6, 2003.

2. See, for example, Joseph S. Nye Jr., *The Paradox of American Power* (New York: Oxford University Press, 2002).

3. Bush, *The National Security Strategy of the United States*, 1.

4. "Bush Announces Combat Operations in Iraq Have Ended," The White House, Office of the Press Secretary, May 1, 2003.

5. "Remarks by National Security Adviser Condoleezza Rice at 28th Annual Convention of the National Association of Black Journalists," The White House, Office of the Press Secretary, August 7, 2003.

6. "President Bush Addresses the Nation Sunday Night," The White House, Office of the Press Secretary, September 7, 2003.

7. Ibid.

8. U.S. Department of Defense, "Quadrennial Defense Review Report," September 30, 2001, 4, http://www.defenselink.mil/pubs/qdr2001.pdf.

About the Author

Thomas Donnelly is a resident fellow in defense and national security studies at the American Enterprise Institute. He is also the author of *Operation Just Cause: The Storming of Panama*; *Clash of Chariots: The Great Tank Battles*; and *Rebuilding America's Defenses: Strategy, Forces and Resources for a New Century*.

Board of Trustees

Bruce Kovner, *Chairman*
Chairman
Caxton Associates, LLC

Lee R. Raymond,
Vice Chairman
Chairman and CEO
Exxon Mobil Corporation

Tully M. Friedman, *Treasurer*
Chairman and CEO
Friedman Fleischer & Lowe LLC

Gordon M. Binder
Managing Director
Coastview Capital, LLC

Harlan Crow
Chairman
Crow Holdings

Christopher DeMuth
President
American Enterprise Institute

Morton H. Fleischer
Chairman and CEO
Spirit Finance Corporation

Christopher B. Galvin
Retired Chairman and CEO
Motorola, Inc.

Raymond V. Gilmartin
Chairman, President, and CEO
Merck & Co., Inc.

Harvey Golub
Chairman and CEO, Retired
American Express Company

Robert F. Greenhill
Chairman
Greenhill & Co., LLC

Roger Hertog
Vice Chairman
Alliance Capital Management
 Corporation

Martin M. Koffel
Chairman and CEO
URS Corporation

John A. Luke Jr.
Chairman and CEO
MeadWestvaco Corporation

L. Ben Lytle
Chairman Emeritus
Anthem, Inc.

Alex J. Mandl
CEO
Gemplus International

Robert A. Pritzker
President and CEO
Colson Associates, Inc.

J. Joe Ricketts
Chairman and Founder
Ameritrade Holding Corporation

George R. Roberts
Kohlberg Kravis Roberts & Co.

The American Enterprise Institute for Public Policy Research

Founded in 1943, AEI is a nonpartisan, nonprofit research and educational organization based in Washington, D.C. The Institute sponsors research, conducts seminars and conferences, and publishes books and periodicals.

AEI's research is carried out under three major programs: Economic Policy Studies; Foreign Policy and Defense Studies; and Social and Political Studies. The resident scholars and fellows listed in these pages are part of a network that also includes ninety adjunct scholars at leading universities throughout the United States and in several foreign countries.

The views expressed in AEI publications are those of the authors and do not necessarily reflect the views of the staff, advisory panels, officers, or trustees.

Kevin B. Rollins
President and COO
Dell, Inc.

John W. Rowe
Chairman and CEO
Exelon Corporation

Edward B. Rust Jr.
Chairman and CEO
State Farm Insurance Companies

William S. Stavropoulos
Chairman and CEO
The Dow Chemical Company

Wilson H. Taylor
Chairman Emeritus
CIGNA Corporation

Marilyn Ware
Chairman Emeritus
American Water

James Q. Wilson
Pepperdine University

Emeritus Trustees

Willard C. Butcher

Richard B. Madden

Robert H. Malott

Paul W. McCracken

Paul F. Oreffice

Henry Wendt

Officers

Christopher DeMuth
President

David Gerson
Executive Vice President

Jason Bertsch
Vice President, Marketing

Montgomery B. Brown
Vice President, Publications

Danielle Pletka
Vice President, Foreign and Defense
Policy Studies

Council of Academic Advisers

James Q. Wilson, *Chairman*
Pepperdine University

Eliot A. Cohen
Professor and Director of Strategic
Studies
School of Advanced International
Studies
Johns Hopkins University

Gertrude Himmelfarb
Distinguished Professor of History
Emeritus
City University of New York

Samuel P. Huntington
Albert J. Weatherhead III
 University Professor of Government
Harvard University

William M. Landes
Clifton R. Musser Professor of Law
 and Economics
University of Chicago Law School

Sam Peltzman
Ralph and Dorothy Keller
Distinguished Service Professor
 of Economics
University of Chicago
 Graduate School of Business

Nelson W. Polsby
Heller Professor of Political Science
Institute of Government Studies
University of California–Berkeley

George L. Priest
John M. Olin Professor of Law and
Economics
Yale Law School

Jeremy Rabkin
Professor of Government
Cornell University

Murray L. Weidenbaum
Mallinckrodt Distinguished
University Professor
Washington University

Richard J. Zeckhauser
Frank Plumpton Ramsey Professor
of Political Economy
Kennedy School of Government
Harvard University

Research Staff

Gautam Adhikari
Visiting Fellow

Joseph Antos
Wilson H. Taylor Scholar in Health
Care and Retirement Policy

Leon Aron
Resident Scholar

Claude E. Barfield
Resident Scholar; Director, Science
and Technology Policy Studies

Roger Bate
Visiting Fellow

Walter Berns
Resident Scholar

Douglas J. Besharov
Joseph J. and Violet Jacobs
Scholar in Social Welfare Studies

Karlyn H. Bowman
Resident Fellow

John E. Calfee
Resident Scholar

Charles W. Calomiris
Arthur F. Burns Scholar in
Economics

Liz Cheney
Visiting Fellow

Lynne V. Cheney
Senior Fellow

Veronique de Rugy
Research Fellow

Thomas Donnelly
Resident Fellow

Nicholas Eberstadt
Henry Wendt Scholar in Political
Economy

Eric M. Engen
Resident Scholar

Mark Falcoff
Resident Scholar

J. Michael Finger
Resident Scholar

Gerald R. Ford
Distinguished Fellow

David Frum
Resident Fellow

Reuel Marc Gerecht
Resident Fellow

Newt Gingrich
Senior Fellow

James K. Glassman
Resident Fellow

Robert A. Goldwin
Resident Scholar

Michael S. Greve
John G. Searle Scholar

Robert W. Hahn
Resident Scholar; Director,
AEI-Brookings Joint Center
for Regulatory Studies

Kevin A. Hassett
Resident Scholar; Director,
Economic Policy Studies

Steven F. Hayward
F. K. Weyerhaeuser Fellow

Robert B. Helms
Resident Scholar; Director,
Health Policy Studies

Frederick M. Hess
Resident Scholar; Director,
Education Policy Studies

R. Glenn Hubbard
Visiting Scholar

Leon R. Kass
Hertog Fellow

Herbert G. Klein
National Fellow

Jeane J. Kirkpatrick
Senior Fellow

Marvin H. Kosters
Resident Scholar

Irving Kristol
Senior Fellow

Randall S. Kroszner
Visiting Scholar

Desmond Lachman
Resident Fellow

Michael A. Ledeen
Freedom Scholar

James R. Lilley
Senior Fellow

Lawrence B. Lindsey
Visiting Scholar

John R. Lott Jr.
Resident Scholar

John H. Makin
Resident Scholar; Director,
Fiscal Policy Studies

Allan H. Meltzer
Visiting Scholar

Joshua Muravchik
Resident Scholar

Charles Murray
W. H. Brady Scholar

Michael Novak
George Frederick Jewett Scholar
in Religion, Philosophy, and Public
Policy; Director, Social and Political
Studies

Norman J. Ornstein
Resident Scholar

Richard Perle
Resident Fellow

Alex J. Pollock
Resident Fellow

Sarath Rajapatirana
Visiting Scholar

Michael Rubin
Resident Scholar

Sally Satel
Resident Scholar

William Schneider
Resident Fellow

Daniel Shaviro
Visiting Scholar

Joel Schwartz
Visiting Scholar

J. Gregory Sidak
Resident Scholar

Radek Sikorski
Resident Fellow; Executive
Director, New Atlantic Initiative

Christina Hoff Sommers
Resident Scholar

Fred Thompson
Visiting Fellow

Peter J. Wallison
Resident Fellow

Scott Wallsten
Resident Scholar

Ben J. Wattenberg
Senior Fellow

John Yoo
Visiting Fellow

Karl Zinsmeister
J. B. Fuqua Fellow; Editor,
The American Enterprise